Relax and Quilt

Oxmoor House®

Relax and Quilt

from the *For the Love of Quilting* series

©1998 by Oxmoor House, Inc.

Book Division of Southern Progress Corporation

P.O. Box 2463, Birmingham, Alabama 35201

Published by Oxmoor House, Inc. and Leisure Arts, Inc.

Library of Congress Catalog Card Number: 98-65846

Hardcover ISBN: 0-8487-1817-8

Softcover ISBN: 0-8487-1818-6

Manufactured in the United States of America

Sixth Printing 2003

Editor-in-Chief: Nancy Fitzpatrick Wyatt

Senior Crafts Editor: Susan Ramey Cleveland

Senior Editor, Editorial Services: Olivia Kindig Wells

Art Director: James Boone

Relax and Quilt

Editor: Patricia Wilens

Copy Editor: Susan S. Cheatham

Associate Art Director: Cynthia R. Cooper

Designer: Emily Albright Parrish

Technical Illustrator: Kelly Davis

Senior Photographer: John O'Hagan

Photo Stylist: Linda Baltzell Wright

Production Director: Phillip Lee

Associate Production Manager: Theresa L. Beste

Production Assistant: Faye Porter Bonner

To order additional publications, call 1-800-633-4910.

For more books to enrich your life,

visit **oxmoorhouse.com**

Relax and Quilt

Edited by Patricia Wilens

Quilt Your Cares Away

Spiral Feathered Star, page 84

For most, stress is a reality of modern life. You're on the run, trying to balance demands of work and family. Face it, sometimes you need a break. You need time for you. Putting together the work of heart, mind, and hands to make a quilt is a great way to relax.

Minutes a Day

"I don't have time" is the usual objection. True, it takes a lot of time to make a quilt. But nowhere is it written that that time has to come in big chunks. Nearly everyone can (and should!) find a few minutes a day to herself. Before breakfast, while the kids are doing homework, whatever.

Use that time to cut a few pieces or put in some stitches. Start small and work toward bigger goals. Set a deadline if you must, but why put that pressure on yourself? A quilt is done when it's done and you'll enjoy it more if you don't stress over it.

Please Yourself

"What if it doesn't come out right?" you worry. And what exactly is "right"? According to whom or what? Your quilt is right if it makes you happy. Unless you submit it for judging in a show, no one is going to examine your quilt for imperfections. Do *you* like the fabrics? Are *you* having fun making it? Are *you* happy with the results? Nobody else's opinion matters one bit.

Get in the Mood

When you're ready to quilt, make it a relaxing time. Put on some music that makes you happy. Or listen to a book-on-tape that carries you off to far-away places. Invite a friend to share the time and the pleasure.

Throughout this book are anecdotes and witticisms from the famous and the humble. Some relate to quiltmaking, others are reflections on life. We hope they make you smile, take your mind off everyday cares, and put you in the mood to quilt.

Have fun. Shake off your worries and inhibitions. Relax. Sip a cup of tea, hum a merry tune, and experience the joy of quilting.

Persuasion, page 34

Summer Sunshine, page 108

Contents

Weekend Wonders

Quick quilts can be fun for beginners and experienced alike.

Rail Fence	10
Birds in the Air	14
Chimneys & Checks	18
Brownies & Pink Lemonade	24
Churn Dash	28

Easy Way Appliqué

Non-traditional methods make appliqué a new adventure.

Persuasion	34
Nifty Note Cards	38
Flowerful Table Runner	42
Coming Up Daisies	44
Daylily	46

Between Friends

Common goals turn quiltmaking into a sharing experience.

Friendship Ribbons	52
Quilt Project Brings Helping Hands to Tornado Victims	55
Rachel's Baskets	56
Chains of Love	60
Buttercream Blues	64

Purely for the Pleasure

Meeting the challenge makes these quilts all the more satisfying.

Baby Baskets	70
Tree of Life	74
Reviving Traditions	80
Spiral Feathered Star	84
Piecing a Curved Seam	88
Bias Appliqué	89
Princess Feathers	90

Breaking Away

Stretch your quilt imagination with creative fabric strategies.

Hummingbird's Delight	98
Star Ripples	102
Summer Sunshine	108
Moon & Star Whimsy	112
Plaid Log Cabin	118

General Instructions

Fabric Preparation	122
Bedcover Size Variations	123
Rotary Cutting	124
Cutting with Templates	126
Machine-Piecing Basics	127
Quick-Piecing Techniques	128
Quick-Pieced Triangle-Squares	130
Traditional Appliqué	131
Joining Blocks	132
Borders	132
Marking a Quilting Design	134
Making a Backing	135
Batting	135
Layering	136
Basting	136
Quilting	137
Tying	137
Binding	139
Hanging Sleeve	141
Care & Cleaning	142
Glossary	143
Mail-Order Resources	144

Buttercream
Blues,
page 64

Weekend Wonders

Hand-work can be therapeutic.

Maybe even engrossing. But quick piecing

is just plain *fun!* Get out your rotary cutter and

mat, fire up the sewing machine, and put

a toe-tapping tune on the stereo—you're

ready for some speedy gratification.

Quick-piecing techniques make these quilts

come together like magic, so they're

ideal starting projects for beginners and a

joy for girls who just want to have fun.

*Didn't this sewing machine help me along fast. I never
mean to sew by hand any more if I can help it.*
*—letter to Anne Whitwell from
her daughter, March 1867*

Birds in the Air,
page 14.

Rail Fence

Enjoy a marathon of strip piecing with friends or in the privacy of your own scrap bag. Nothing is faster or more fun than this quilt that's as easy as 1-2-3. Three strips of fabric, that is. The piecing is even easier if you use consistent fabrics instead of scraps. This is the ideal project for beginners or for experienced quiltmakers in a hurry.

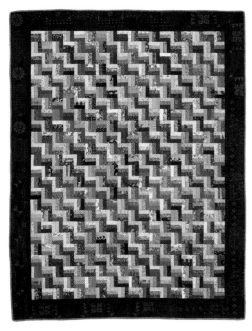

Finished Size: 66" x 84"
Blocks: 432 (3" x 3")

Rail Fence Block—Make 432.

Materials

2¼ yards outer border fabric*
½ yard inner border fabric*
216 (1½" x 21") cross-grain strips for piecing (72 *each* of light, medium, and dark fabrics)
⅞ yard binding fabric
2 yards 90"-wide backing fabric
*Note: Cut border strips; then add leftover fabric to scraps for piecing.

Cutting

Instructions are for strip cutting and quick piecing. Cut all strips cross-grain (except borders). Cut pieces in order listed to get most efficient use of yardage.

From outer border fabric, cut:
2 (5" x 78") and 2 (5" x 70") lengthwise strips.

From inner border fabric, cut:
8 (2"-wide) strips for inner border.

Making Blocks

See page 129 for illustrated instructions for strip piecing.

1. Before piecing, sort fabric strips into color families. Group blues together; then reds, browns, etc.
2. For first strip set, select a light, a medium, and a dark strip from 1 color family. Join strips as shown (*Strip Set Diagram*). Press seam allowances toward center strip.
3. Cut strip set into 6 (3½"-wide) segments as shown. Presto! You've already made 6 blocks. Isn't it easy?
4. Repeat with remaining strips to make a total of 432 blocks. ⟶

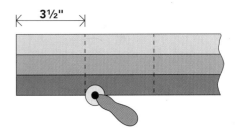

3½"

Strip Set Diagram

Laugh and the world laughs with you;
Weep, and you weep alone;
For the sad old earth must borrow its mirth,
But has trouble enough of its own.
—Ella Wheeler Wilcox, American poet, 1855-1919

Quilt Assembly

1. Referring to photo, lay out blocks in 24 horizontal rows of 18 blocks each *(Row Assembly Diagram)*. For Row 1 and all odd-numbered rows, first block is horizontal with light strip at top; then alternate blocks vertically and horizontally as shown. For Row 2 and all even-numbered rows, first block is vertical with light strip at left; then alternate horizontal and vertical blocks as shown.

2. When satisfied with block placement, join blocks in each row.

3. Join rows.

Borders

1. Join 2 strips of inner border fabric end-to-end to make a border strip for each quilt side.

2. Referring to page 132, measure quilt from top to bottom through middle of quilt. Trim 2 border strips to match length. Sew border strips to quilt sides. Press seam allowances toward borders.

3. Measure quilt from side to side through middle of quilt. Trim remaining border strips to match quilt width. Sew trimmed borders to top and bottom edges. Press seam allowances toward borders.

4. Repeat steps 2 and 3 to add outer border strips to quilt sides.

Quilting and Finishing

1. Mark quilting design on quilt top as desired. On quilt shown, patchwork is outline-quilted and border is stipple-quilted by machine.

2. Layer backing, batting, and quilt top. Baste. Quilt as desired.

3. Make 8⅝ yards of binding. See page 139 for instructions on making and applying binding.

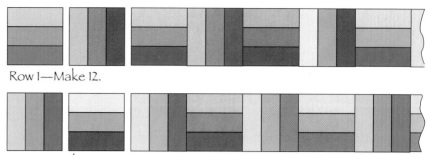

Row 1—Make 12.

Row 2—Make 12.

Row Assembly Diagram

Quilt by Kitty Sorgen of Newbury Park, California, for Riad Alameddine of Lafayette, California

Bits and Pieces

Lessons in Quilting

My son taught me an important quilting lesson. When he was 20 years old, Dan gave me a gift certificate for a quilting class. With my newfound skills, I offered to mend the tattered little quilt he'd been dragging around since he was 5. Made from scraps by a Waco, Texas, ladies' group, that quilt had endured hard use and countless washings.

But Danny snatched the quilt from me and held it tight to his chest, spurning my offer to make the quilt "good as new." "You don't understand," Danny said. "Nothing you can do to this quilt will make it better than it already is. My life is in this quilt." He recounted boyhood memories of using the quilt as a tent, to wrap up with his dog when he'd had a bad day, or when he was sick. Even now, a grown man and a father, Dan keeps that little quilt—not to use, but just to have. I can only hope that the quilts I make are precious enough to be loved to shreds.

—Kitty Sorgen
Newbury Park, California

If you ever have a new idea, and it's really new, you have to expect that it won't be widely accepted immediately. It's a long, hard process. —Physicist Rosalyn Yallow

No Time Like the Present

I used to try to block out time for quilting but was always interrupted. Then, when I was caring for my terminally ill uncle, he told me that my grandmother was a quilter. She was a farm wife and mother of 10 who died at age 44. How did she have time to quilt? Uncle said she would put in just a few stitches between other tasks. Now I've learned to take advantage of small bits of time. Even if I only get in a few stitches, those are still more stitches than I started the day with.

—Marjean Sargent, Malvern, Iowa

Everything's Better with Friends

When I get together with quilting friends, we talk about everything. No topic is off-limits. We all go home feeling better for having been together.

—Kitty Sorgen, Newbury Park, California

Not Such a Bargain After All

I once saved $2 by buying three bags of pony beads for a project. Since I had 500 beads, I didn't worry when a couple of beads rolled off the table and I couldn't find them.

Well, we found them all right. In the poor cat's tummy! Tim is a very loud cat. When I noticed he wasn't up to his usual moaning and groaning, I knew something was wrong. Several X-rays and an operation later, the vet extracted two pony beads. I told the vet I had no idea where the cat found them. (I just know I'm going to roast for telling lies!) Tim is his old loud self again, and I have a $200 vet's bill to offset the "bargain" on the beads.

—Terry Benzo, Pittsburgh, Pennsylvania

Birds in the Air

Quick-pieced triangle-squares make this a fun quilt-top-in-a-long-weekend. If you're in a hurry or just taking it easy, enjoy cleaning out the scrap bag and mixing it up.

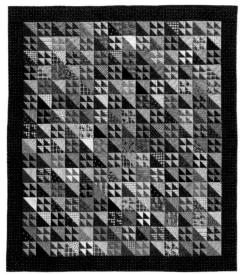

Finished Size: 64" x 72"
Blocks: 56 (8" x 8")

Birds in the Air Block—Make 56.

Materials

56 (5") squares dark scraps
56 (5") squares medium/light scraps
112 (5" x 7¾") dark scraps
112 (5" x 7¾") medium/light scraps
2 yards border fabric (includes binding)
4 yards backing fabric

I wasn't allowed to speak when my husband was alive, and since he's been gone no one has been able to shut me up. —Hedda Hopper

Unit A

1. On wrong side of each light 5" square, draw a diagonal line through center of square *(Unit A Diagram)*.
2. Match each marked square with a dark square, right sides facing. Stitch on both sides of diagonal line as shown.
3. Cut on drawn line to separate 2 triangle-squares. Press seam allowances toward dark fabric.
4. Make 112 of Unit A (2 for each block), varying fabric combinations as desired.

Unit B

See page 130 for illustrated step-by-step instructions for sewing quick-pieced triangle-squares.
1. On wrong side of each light 5" x 7¾" piece, mark a 1-square by 2-square grid of 2⅞" squares as shown *(Unit B Diagram)*.
2. Stitch grid as shown. Press. Cut on all drawn lines to get 4 matching triangle-squares. Press seam allowances toward dark fabric.
3. Join 4 matching triangle-squares as shown to make 112 of Unit B (2 for each block).

Block Assembly

1. For each block, select 2 each of units A and B.
2. Lay out units in 2 rows *(Block Assembly Diagram)*, positioning each unit with dark half of triangle-square(s) at bottom. Join units in 2 rows. Press joining seam allowances toward Unit A in each row.
3. Join rows to complete block.
4. Make 56 blocks.

Quilt Assembly

Referring to photo on page 16, lay out blocks in 8 horizontal rows with 7 blocks in each row. When satisfied with block placement, join blocks in each row. For ease of assembly, press joining seam allowances in one direction in even-numbered rows and in opposite direction in odd-numbered rows. Then join rows. $\longrightarrow$

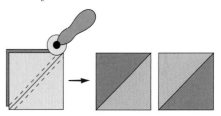

Unit A—Make 112.

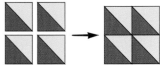

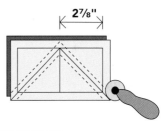

Unit B—Make 112.

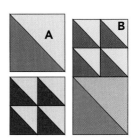

Block Assembly Diagram

Borders

1. From border fabric, cut 4 (4½" x 67") strips.

2. Referring to page 132, measure quilt from top to bottom through middle of quilt. Trim 2 strips to match length. Sew trimmed border strips to quilt sides. Press seam allowances toward borders.

3. Measure quilt from side to side through middle of quilt. Trim remaining borders to match quilt width. Sew trimmed borders to top and bottom edges. Press seam allowances toward borders.

Quilting and Finishing

1. Mark quilting design on quilt top as desired. On quilt shown, Carole Collins hand-quilted diagonal lines in each Unit A and outline-quilted triangles in Unit B.

2. Divide backing fabric into 2 equal lengths. See page 135 for instructions on making a backing.

3. Layer backing, batting, and quilt top, with backing seams parallel to top and bottom edges of quilt. Baste. Quilt as desired.

4. Use remaining border fabric to make 7⅞ yards of binding. See page 139 for instructions on making and applying binding.

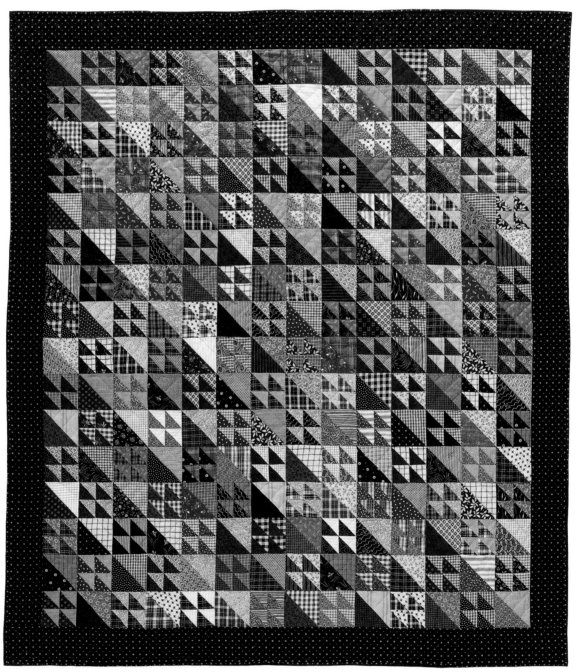

Quilt by Carole Collins of Norfolk, Nebraska

Historic Quilt Becomes Symbol of Kindness

The pioneers who settled the American West brought with them quilts that were precious mementos and necessary bedcoverings. But once, a little quilt from back East became a symbol of trust and kindness between strangers.

Emma Bradbury, a young widow with a little daughter, traveled by train from Connecticut to Ohio and then set off in a wagon on her own to join her parents in Kansas. It was a dangerous undertaking for a woman alone, but Emma was no ordinary woman.

Travelling through the sea of grass that was the Midwestern plain, one day Emma saw a lone Indian in the distance. He beckoned the wagon to come closer. Emma approached with rifle in hand, wondering why he seemed so agitated. He led her to a stand of trees where she found the man's wife about to give birth.

After Emma helped the girl deliver a healthy son, she wrapped the baby in a little quilt that she had made as a gift for her nephew. Though she had worked long and hard on the red and yellow pieces, the child's need was great.

That night, Emma cared for the Indian family in her wagon. Why were they all alone, she wondered. Where were they from?

In the morning, the young man led the wagon to a nearby village.

Emma's fear at being surrounded by Indians soon vanished. Despite lack of a common language, she understood their gratitude. The wagon was soon loaded with gifts from the grateful Indians, who sent Emma on her way with smiles.

But before she left, Emma found a scrap of paper and wrote on it her name and the town where she was heading. She gave the paper to the husband, who was clearly mystified by it. As Emma drove off, she wondered why on earth she had done such a thing.

Emma reached Kansas safely. She remarried and raised a family. On a day more than 22 years after her Indian adventure, Emma's husband called her from the house with the news that an Indian had come to town, showing a paper with Emma's name on it.

In the street, a tall young man greeted Emma. "I am Clear Water," he said. "If you are Emma Bradbury, then you brought me into this world. Now it is fitting that I bring my own son for you to see." Emma's heart swelled as she took the child in her arms, for he was wrapped in the little quilt she had made so many years before.

For the Indian family had lovingly cared for her quilt as a symbol of kindness and the universal love of a child.

Original story told by M.L. Kitsen, descendant of Emma's friend, Louisa Christy.

Time-Saving Tips

Make the most of a few spare minutes to take care of little chores. Wind bobbins, thread needles, make a few templates. When you have an hour or two to really concentrate on sewing, these start-up chores will be out of the way and you're ready to go.

❖

Tip for Strips
Don't just fold up leftover fabric. If there's just a little fabric left, I cut it into 1½"-wide strips and save them up. Before I know it, I have enough strips for a fun Log Cabin or Rail Fence quilt and the strips are already cut. —Lila Taylor Scott, Marietta, Georgia

Soul Food

When nights are cold and you need an extra cover, a store-bought blanket will stop your shivers, but a handmade quilt warms the soul.
—Bonnie Leman

Quilting is my creative outlet. And I have a lot of outlets in my house.
—Judie Herzog, Fairfield, Iowa

Chimneys & Checks

The crisp, bold contrast of black and white provides the perfect background for easy-to-sew rails of bright jewel-tone fabrics. Use coordinating prints and solids to create the light/dark striped effect of this quick-piecing delight, or get creative with scrap fabrics if you prefer.

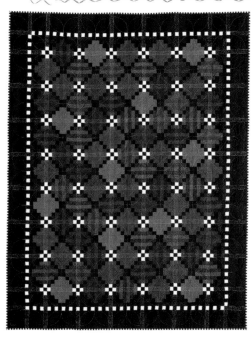

Finished Size: 66½" x 88½"
Blocks: 48 (9" x 9")

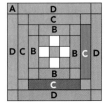

Corner Block—Make 4.

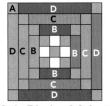

Side Block—Make 20.

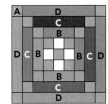

Center Block—Make 24.

Materials

3 yards black*
½ yard white
¼ yard *each* 7 dark solids and
    7 coordinating tone-on-tone prints
¾ yard binding fabric
2 yards 90"-wide backing fabric
*Note: Use more than 1 fabric, if
    desired. Quilt shown uses black
    solid and a black tone-on-tone
    print. Varied scrap fabrics will also
    work. However, we recommend A
    squares be uniform for best effect.

Cutting

Instructions are for strip cutting and quick piecing. Cut all strips cross-grain (except borders). Cut pieces in order listed to get most efficient use of yardage.

From black, cut:
2 (5½" x 78") and 2 (5½" x 70")
    lengthwise strips for border.
13 (1½"-wide) strips for strip sets 1
    and 2.
54 (1½" x 22") strips. From these, cut
    576 (1½") A squares. Save remain-
    ing strips for block piecing.

From white, cut:
11 (1½"-wide) strips for strip sets 1
    and 2.

**From *each* coordinating solid and
print fabric, cut:**
5 (1½"-wide) strips.

Planning Ahead

This variation of the Chimneys & Cornerstones block is easy to sew, but it takes planning to achieve the overall design. Use the *Planning Diagram,* page 20, to map out blocks so you can enjoy sewing without worrying about what fabric goes where. Make several photo-copies of the diagram to try differ-ent arrangements.

The diagram shows all the blocks, numbered by row. Each block is visually divided into quad-rants around the center nine-patch.

Sort fabrics into 7 color groups. You should have 5 strips each of a dark solid and a print fabric in each color group. Get a colored pencil to represent each group.

Let's say one pencil is red. Select any quadrant on the diagram, on any block, and color it red. Then color the *adjacent* quadrant in the *adjacent* block red also, making a diamond. Repeat 11 times, spacing 12 red units around the quilt. Repeat with each color until you've filled in all spaces. (*Note:* Last 2 colors will have only 11 units each.)

Once you're happy with your colored schematic, use it as a guide as you sew the blocks, matching fabrics in neighboring quadrants.

$\longrightarrow$

I have everything I had 20 years ago, only it's all a little bit lower.
—Gypsy Rose Lee

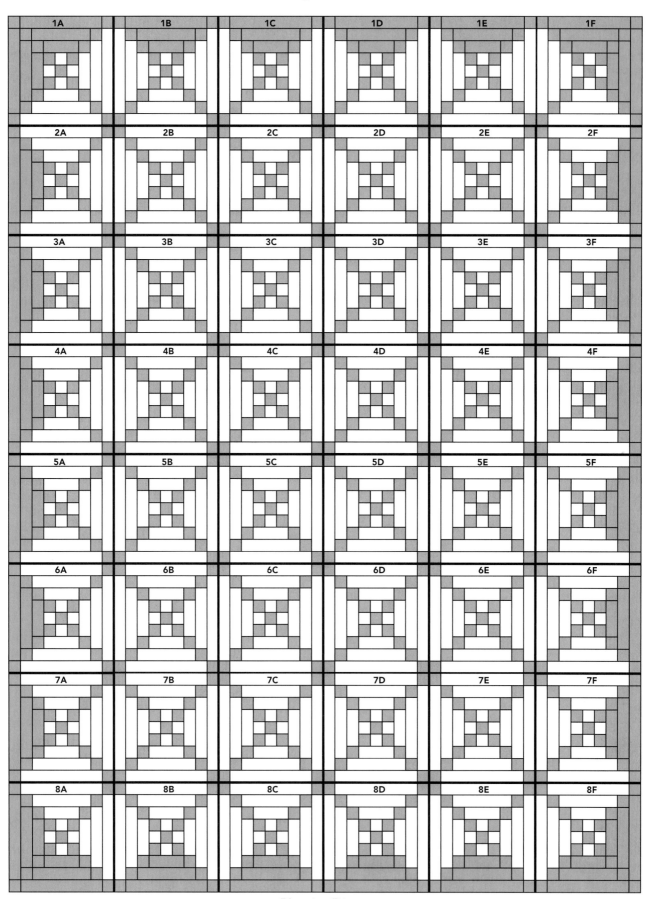

Planning Diagram

Nine-Patches

For this quilt, we recommend making one block at a time, following the numbered blocks on your quilt schematic. This will help you keep fabric placement in order. Some initial steps, however, will enable you to quick-piece the nine-patch units used in all blocks.

See page 129 for illustrated instructions for strip piecing.

1. For Strip Set 1, select 2 black strips and 1 white strip. Join strips as shown *(Strip Set 1 Diagram)*. Make 5 of Strip Set 1. Press seam allowances toward black.

2. For Strip Set 2, select 1 black strip and 2 white strips. Join strips as shown *(Strip Set 2 Diagram)*. Make 3 of Strip Set 2. Press seam allowances toward black.

3. Cut strip sets into 1½"-wide segments. Cut 96 Strip Set 1 segments and 48 Strip Set 2 segments for block nine-patches. Set aside remainder of strip sets for border.

4. Join a Strip Set 1 segment to both sides of each Strip Set 2 segment to make 48 nine-patches *(Diagram A)*.

Corner Blocks

For this method, cut pieces for individual rails only as directed.

1. For Block 1A, select 1 black strip, 12 black A squares, and 1 strip each of designated fabrics, according to your colored Planning Diagram.

2. Strips are sewn to opposite sides of nine-patch in alphabetical order. For first B rail, match colored fabric strip to nine-patch, right sides facing, and stitch *(Diagram B)*. Trim strip even with bottom of nine-patch. Press seam allowance toward B.

3. Repeat with black strip on opposite side of nine-patch *(Diagram C)*.

4. Cut 3½" lengths of black and next colored fabric. Sew A squares to both ends of each piece *(Diagram D)*. Press seam allowances toward squares. Stitch units to top and bottom edges of block *(Diagram E)*.

5. For C rails, sew strips of black and color to sides of block as before. Then add A squares to 5½" strips of black and color and sew those strips to top and bottom edges *(Diagram F)*.

6. Complete last round of D rails around block in same manner, cutting 7½" strips of black and color.

7. Repeat Corner Block procedure to make blocks 1F, 8A, and 8F.

Side & Center Blocks

Blocks for sides and center are made in same manner as Corner Block, starting with a nine-patch. Refer to diagrams A–F, as well as schematic and block diagrams, for correct color placement. Alternate dark and medium fabrics as you sew each block.

1. For Block 1B, select 1 nine-patch, 12 A squares, 1 black strip, 1 strip each of fabrics to match adjacent edge of Block 1A, and 1 strip each of 2 other designated color groups.

2. Follow Side Block diagram to make blocks around outside edge of quilt (except corner blocks).

3. Follow Center Block diagram and schematic to make 24 interior blocks, using 4 color fabrics. $\longrightarrow$

1½"

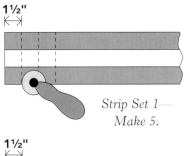

*Strip Set 1—
Make 5.*

1½"

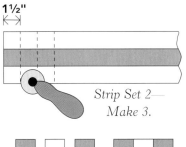

*Strip Set 2—
Make 3.*

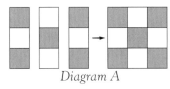

Diagram A

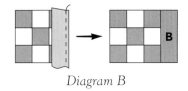

Diagram B

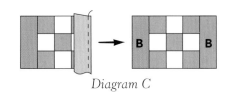

Diagram C

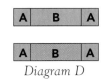

Diagram D

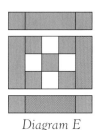

Diagram E

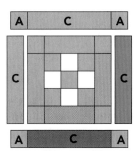

Diagram F

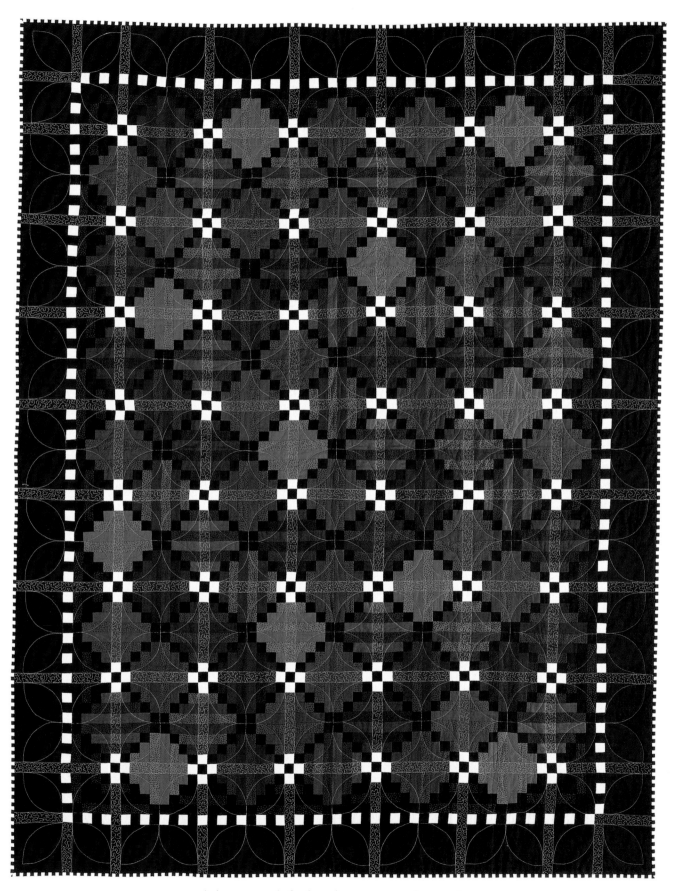

Quilt by Mimi Alef of High Point, North Carolina

Quilt Assembly

1. Lay out blocks in 8 horizontal rows of 6 blocks each, referring to photo, schematic, and *Row Assembly Diagram*. Be sure fabrics align correctly in adjacent blocks. Resew blocks that do not match properly.
2. When satisfied with block placement, join blocks in each row.
3. Join rows.

Borders

1. Cut 44 (1½"-wide) segments of Strip Set 1 and 42 (1½"-wide) segments of Strip Set 2 for border.
2. For left side border, select 12 of each segment type. Join 24 segments end-to-end, alternating segment types along row. Sew border strip to side of quilt with Strip Set 1 unit at upper left corner of quilt. Ease border to quilt as necessary.
3. Assemble right side border in same manner. Sew border strip to quilt, positioning Strip Set 2 segment at upper right corner of quilt.
4. For top border, select 10 segments of Strip Set 1 and 9 of Strip Set 2. Starting with a #1 segment, join segments end-to-end as before.
5. Use a seam ripper to remove last black square from one end of border strip, leaving white square at end of strip. Referring to photo, match border to top edge of quilt with white square at upper left corner. Stitch border in place, easing as necessary.
6. Assemble bottom border in same manner, this time starting with a Strip Set 2 segment. Remove a black square from last #1 segment before sewing it to end of row.

7. Referring to photo, match border to bottom edge of quilt, with white square at bottom right corner. Sew border in place, easing as necessary.
8. Referring to page 132, measure quilt from top to bottom through middle of quilt. Trim 2 black border strips to match length. Sew border strips to quilt sides. Press seam allowances toward borders.
9. Measure quilt from side to side through middle of quilt. Trim remaining black borders to match quilt width. Sew trimmed borders to top and bottom edges. Press seam allowances toward borders.

Quilting and Finishing

1. Mark quilting design on quilt top as desired. Quilt shown has straight bands of stipple quilting running through center of each block, connecting nine-patches and extending into solid border. Squares formed by stippled bands are quilted in a melon-patch design. Mimi Alef used silver metallic thread for machine quilting.
2. Layer backing, batting, and quilt top. Baste. Quilt as desired.
3. Make 8⅝ yards of straight-grain binding. See page 139 for instructions on making and applying binding.

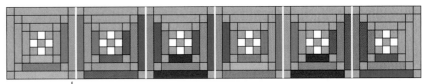

Row 1—Make 2.

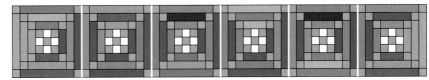

Row 2—Make 6.

Row Assembly Diagram

He that is of merry heart hath a continual feast.

—Proverbs 15:15

Brownies & Pink Lemonade

Quilters like to sew with good friends, good conversation, and good food. This quick quilt fills the bill with easy, scrappy piecing. Choose colors for your variation of the Mosaic block that remind you of favorite things. When Kitty Sorgen chose these fabrics, she was thinking chocolate . . . yummmm.

Finished Size: 63½" x 77"
Blocks: 12 (12½" x 12½")

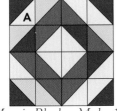

Mosaic Block—Make 12.

Materials

24 (10" x 14") brown, dark red scraps
24 (10") squares pink, cream scraps
15 (5¾") squares pink, cream scraps
⅜ yard inner border fabric
2⅜ yards outer border fabric*
¾ yard binding fabric
4 yards backing fabric
*Note: Border fabric shown is a stripe that gives the appearance of multiple borders. If this type of fabric is not available at your local stores, consult mail-order sources listed on page 144.

Making Blocks

See page 130 for illustrated step-by-step instructions on sewing quick-pieced triangle-squares.

1. On wrong side of each light 10" square, draw a 2-square by 2-square grid of 4" squares *(Diagram A)*. Draw diagonal lines through center of each square as shown.

2. From each brown or red fabric, cut a 10" square. (Set remainder aside for pieced border.) Match each square with a marked light square, right sides facing.

3. Stitch on both sides of diagonal lines as shown. Blue line on diagram shows first continuous stitching path; red line shows second continuous path.

4. Cut on drawn lines to separate triangle-squares. Cut 8 A triangle-squares from each grid to get a total of 192 for blocks. Press seam allowances toward darker fabric.

5. Select any 4 triangle-squares, including at least 1 with a red triangle. Join squares in pairs; then join pairs to make quarter-block unit, placing red triangle in outside corner as shown *(Diagram B)*. Make 48 quarter-block units, mixing scrap fabrics as much as possible.

6. Select any 4 quarter-block units. Join units in pairs, keeping red in uter corners *(Block Assembly Diagram)*. Press; then join pairs to complete block.

7. Make 12 blocks.

Quilt Assembly

Referring to photo, lay out blocks in 4 horizontal rows with 3 blocks in each row. When satisfied with block placement, join blocks in each row. For ease of assembly, press joining seam allowances in one direction in even-numbered rows and in opposite direction in odd-numbered rows. Then join rows. $\longrightarrow$

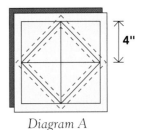

Diagram A

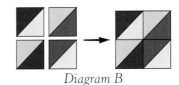

Diagram B

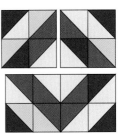

Block Assembly Diagram

Pleasures are like poppies spread. —Robert Burns

Borders

1. From inner border fabric, cut 4 (2"-wide) cross-grain strips. Join 2 strips for each side border.

2. Referring to page 132, measure quilt from top to bottom through middle of quilt. Trim border strips to match length. Sew trimmed strips to quilt sides. Press seam allowances toward borders.

3. For top and bottom borders, cut 2 (2½"-wide) cross-grain strips. (Note these are a little wider than side borders.) Measure quilt from side to side through middle of quilt. Trim borders to match quilt width. Sew trimmed borders to top and bottom edges. Press seam allowances toward borders.

4. Cut 13 (5¾") light squares in quarters diagonally to get 50 B triangles (and 2 extra). From remaining brown/red scraps, cut 38 (3⅝") C squares and 4 (3⅝" x 6¾") D corner pieces.

5. For top border, select 16 B triangles and 8 C squares. Join triangles to opposite sides of 7 squares (Diagram C). Press seam allowances toward squares. Sew 2 remaining triangles to adjacent sides of last square (Diagram D).

6. Join units in a row (Diagram E). Sew assembled border to top edge of quilt, easing to fit as needed.

7. Make bottom border in same manner and join to quilt edge.

8. For each side border, select 22 B triangles and 11 C squares. Join Bs and Cs as before; then join units in a row. Sew borders to quilt sides, easing to fit as needed.

9. Sew a B triangle to short sides of each D rectangle (Diagram F). Press seam allowances toward D. Cut remaining 5¾" light squares in half diagonally to get 4 E corner triangles; then join triangles to bottom of D to complete corner unit. (Triangles are cut large; trim as needed.)

10. Sew corner units to border corners as shown (Diagram G).

11. Cut 4 (7¼" x 84") lengthwise strips of outer border fabric. Referring to page 133, join borders to quilt and miter corners.

Quilting and Finishing

1. Mark quilting design on quilt top as desired. Quilt shown is outline-quilted with a flower quilted in C squares (see pattern below).

2. Divide backing fabric into 2 equal lengths. See page 135 for instructions on making a backing.

3. Layer backing, batting, and quilt top. Baste. Quilt as desired.

4. Make 8 yards of binding. See page 139 for instructions on making and applying binding.

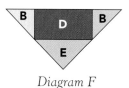

Diagram F

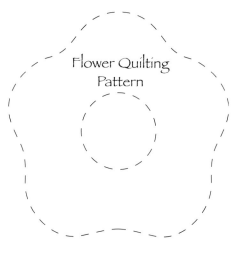

Flower Quilting Pattern

A new friend is as new wine: when it is old, thou shalt drink it with pleasure.
—Ecclesiasticus 9:10

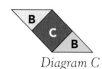

Diagram C

Diagram D

Diagram G

Diagram E

Quilt by Kitty Sorgen of Newbury Park, California;
hand-quilted by Suzanne Devine

Churn Dash

This block is also known as Monkey Wrench, Shoo Fly, or Hole-in-the-Barn Door, but by any other name this quilt is just as intriguing. Blocks seem to appear within blocks, and how does it all go together? Clever sashing does the trick, along with a slap of quick-pieced triangle-squares and a dash of strip piecing.

Finished Size: 42½" x 42½"
Blocks: 24 (6" x 6")

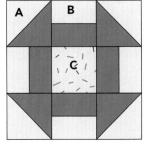

Churn Dash Block—Make 24.

Materials

12 (10½" x 14½") print scraps for blocks (4 *each* green, red, blue)
12 (10½" x 14½") assorted light scraps for blocks
3 (2½" x 21") strips light prints for block centers
¼ yard red print for sashing squares
⅛ yard *each* green, red, and blue prints for sashing
⅛ yard each 10 assorted light fabrics for sashing
⅝ yard binding fabric
1⅜ yards backing fabric

Making Blocks

See page 130 for illustrated step-by-step instructions for quick-pieced triangle-squares. See page 129 for tips on strip piecing.

1. From each 10½" x 14½" piece, cut a 7½" square and 2 (1½" x 10") strips. Set aside remainder of these fabrics for sashing.

2. On wrong side of each light 7½" square, draw a 2-square by 2-square grid of 2⅞" squares *(Diagram A)*. Draw diagonal lines through center of each square as shown.

3. Match each marked square with a dark square, right sides facing.

4. Stitch on both sides of diagonal lines as shown. Blue line on diagram shows first continuous stitching path; red shows second path.

5. Cut on drawn lines to separate triangle-squares. Cut 8 A triangle-squares from each grid. Press seam allowances toward darker fabric.

6. Sort pairs of light and dark 1½" x 10" strips, matching same fabrics as for triangle-squares.

7. Join strips *(Diagram B)*. Press; then cut 4 (2½"-wide) B segments from each strip set as shown.

8. Cut 8 (2½") C squares from each fabric for block centers.

9. For each block, select 4 matching A triangle-squares, 4 B units, and 1 C square. Lay out units in 3 horizontal rows *(Block Assembly Diagram)*. Join units in each row. Press seam allowances away from B units. Join rows to complete block.

10. Make 24 blocks. ⟶

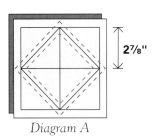

Diagram A

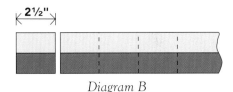

Diagram B

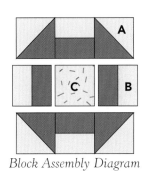

Block Assembly Diagram

The playful kitten . . . is infinitely more amusing than half the people one is obliged to live with in the world.

—Lady Sydney Morgan, English writer, 1783–1859

Sashing Units

1. Cut 3 (1½"-wide) cross-grain strips from green sashing fabric. Cut 3 strips of a light fabric to match.
2. Join 2 strips as shown *(Strip Set 1 Diagram)*. Make 3 of Strip Set 1. Press seam allowances toward green. From these strip sets, cut 36 (2½"-wide) B sashing segments.
3. Repeat Step 1 with blue and red sashing fabrics *(Strip Set Diagrams)*. From each of these strip sets, cut 32 (2½"-wide) B segments for sashing.
4. Cut 25 (2½") C squares from red print fabric.
5. Sew matching B units to opposite sides of each square, with dark fabric to outside *(Diagram C)*. Make 25 Sashing Units.
6. From remaining light fabrics, cut 64 (2½") C squares. Then cut 14 (4") squares; cut these in quarters diagonally to get 56 D triangles.
7. From fabrics leftover from blocks, cut 8 (2⅞") squares of light fabrics

and 8 dark squares. On wrong side of light square, draw a diagonal line *(Diagram D)*. Match light and dark squares, right sides facing. Stitch on both sides of diagonal line. Cut 2 triangle-squares apart on drawn line. Make 16 A triangle-squares.
8. Sew 2 D triangles to sides of each triangle-square *(Border Unit Diagram)*. Press seam allowances toward triangles. Make 16 Border Units.
9. From light scraps, cut 2 (2¼") squares. Cut squares in half diagonally to get 4 E corner triangles.

Quilt Assembly

Follow *Quilt Assembly Diagram* to lay out blocks and sashing units in diagonal rows. Working on a clean floor or a large table, start laying out units with bottom left corner of quilt. Do not join units until all rows are laid out and you are satisfied with placement.

1. For Row 1, select 2 Border Units. Between these units, line up 1 each of units B, C, and E as shown.
2. For Row 2, select 1 Sashing Unit with fabrics that match B unit in Row 1. Stack C squares and D triangles at both ends of Sashing Unit as shown.
3. For Row 3, select any 2 blocks, 2 Border Units, 3 C squares, 2 D triangles and 4 B units (1 of which matches fabrics in Row 2 Sashing Unit). Lay out units as shown.

Strip Set 1—Make 3.
Strip Set 2—Make 3.
Strip Set 3—Make 3.

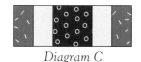
Diagram C

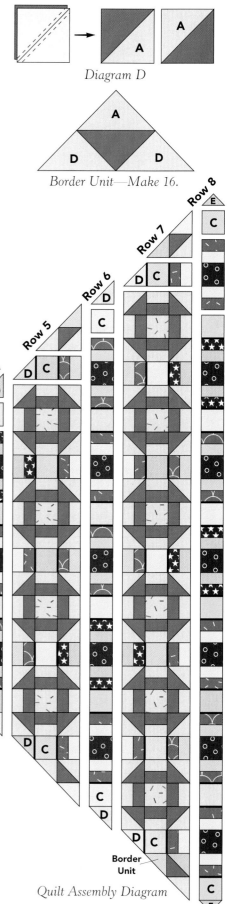
Diagram D
Border Unit—Make 16.
Quilt Assembly Diagram

4. Continue selecting units for each row as shown, being careful to match adjacent Bs and Sashing Units that make secondary blocks when rows are joined.

5. When units are laid out for rows 1–8, stand back and take stock of layout. Change color placement as desired. Row 8 is center row of quilt—to continue with top half of quilt, turn diagram around and work out from Row 8 toward upper right corner of quilt.

6. Check position of all units. When satisifed, join units in each row.

7. Lay out rows again to check position. (It's important for everything to be placed correctly for design to work.) Make any changes needed; then join rows.

Quilting and Finishing

1. Mark quilting design on quilt top as desired. Quilt shown is outline-quilted.

2. Layer backing, batting, and quilt top. Baste. Quilt as desired.

3. Make 5 yards of binding. See page 139 for instructions on making and applying binding.

Quilt by Mary Carole Sternitzky Knapp of Garfield, Arkansas

Easy Way Appliqué

Everybody loves the look of appliqué, but not everyone likes *doing* it. If you can't make peace with freezer paper or turned edges, explore alternative methods that eliminate pesky seam allowances—making appliqué fast, fun, and easy for everyone. You can use these patterns for traditional appliqué, but try the easy way for a new adventure.

The country demands bold, persistent experimentation. It is common sense to take a method and try it. If it fails . . . try another. But above all, try something.
—Franklin D. Roosevelt

Flowerful Table Runner,
page 42

Persuasion

When you dare to stray from tradition, go all out! This wall hanging starts with easy four-patch blocks in scrap fabrics, but the border throws caution to the wind. We call it "free-form appliqué"—no patterns, no seam allowances, no rules at all. You'll have great fun creating all manner of doo-dads to make your border unique. And it's so easy to sew, it makes appliqué a real joy.

Finished Size: 52" x 52"
Blocks: 25 (5¾" x 5¾")

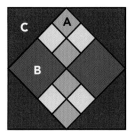

Improved Four-Patch Block—Make 25.

> Being an old maid is like death by drowning—a really delightful sensation after you haved ceased struggling. —Edna Ferber

Materials

1⅝ yards teal
1 yard green (includes binding)
½ yard red
Assorted scraps for piecing and
    appliqué (approximately 8" x 10"
    pieces of 24 or more fabrics)
3 yards backing fabric
⅜"-wide bias pressing bar
Black and white embroidery floss or
    pearl cotton

Cutting

Cut pieces in order listed to make best use of yardage. When pieces listed below are cut, add scraps to fabrics for blocks and appliqué.

From teal, cut:
4 (6¾" x 56") lengthwise strips for
    borders.
60 (1½" x 6¼") sashing strips.

From green, cut:
20" square for bias vine.
5 (2½"-wide) cross-grain strips for
    binding.

From red, cut:
4 (2½" x 40") strips for inner border.

Making Blocks

1. Cut a 1½" x 6" strip from each of 2 fabrics. Join strips in a strip set *(Diagram A)*. Press seam allowances toward darker fabric.
2. Cut strip set into 4 (1½"-wide) A segments as shown.
3. Join segments in pairs to make 2 four-patch units *(Diagram B)*.
4. From another scrap, cut 2 (2½") B squares. Join these with four-patches to complete center unit *(Diagram C)*.

5. Cut 2 (3¾") squares of another fabric. Cut each square in half diagonally to get 4 C triangles.
6. Center C triangles on 2 opposite sides of center unit, leaving triangle "ears" on either side *(Block Assembly Diagram)*. Press seam allowances toward triangles. Then sew triangles to remaining sides to complete block.
7. Make 25 Improved Four-Patch blocks in this manner, using scraps as desired. Set aside remaining scraps for appliqué. ⟶

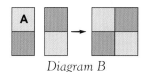

Diagram A

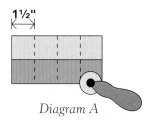

Diagram B

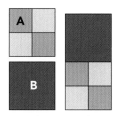

Diagram C

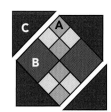

Block Assembly Diagram

Quilt Assembly

1. Lay out 6 rows of sashing strips as shown *(Row Assembly Diagram)*. From assorted scraps, cut 36 (1½") sashing squares. Fill in sashing squares between sashing strips and at row ends as shown.

2. Lay out blocks in 5 horizontal rows of 5 blocks each, placing remaining sashing strips between blocks and at row ends as shown. Rearrange blocks to get a nice balance of fabrics, color, and value.

3. When satisfied with placement, join blocks and sashing strips in each block row. Join sashing strips and squares in each sashing row.

4. Join rows.

Borders

1. Referring to page 132, measure quilt from top to bottom through middle of quilt. Trim 2 red border strips to match length. Sew these to quilt sides. Press seam allowances toward borders.

2. Measure quilt from side to side through middle of quilt. Trim remaining red borders to match quilt width. Sew trimmed borders to top and bottom edges. Press seam allowances toward borders.

3. Referring to page 133, sew teal borders to quilt. Miter corners.

Appliqué

1. Referring to page 139, cut 5¼ yards of 1¼"-wide continuous bias from 20" green square. See page 89 for instructions on preparing bias for appliqué. Sew and press a continuous length of ⅜"-wide bias for vine.

2. Starting at center of any side, pin vine on teal border in an unplanned meandering wiggle. Use matching thread to hand-appliqué vine in place. Don't worry about finishing bias ends—these will be covered

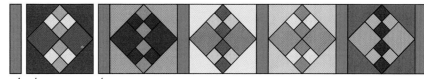

Sashing Row—Make 6.

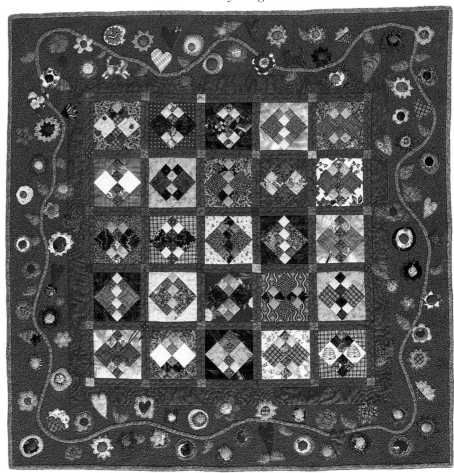

Block Row—Make 5.

Row Assembly Diagram

Quilt by Patricia Wilens of Birmingham, Alabama
Machine-quilted by Lynn Witzenburg of Des Moines, Iowa

with doo-dads later.

3. From scraps, cut assorted leaves, flowers, and other shapes for appliqué. We've provided some patterns to get you started (page 37), but it's more fun to cut pieces freehand. On quilt shown, no 2 pieces are alike and hearts are asymmetrical because they were cut freestyle. Some doo-dads are just circles. For method shown, do not add seam allowances. For traditional hand

appliqué, add seam allowances and prepare pieces for appliqué as described on page 131.

4. Referring to photo, pin appliqués on border as desired. Layer pieces on top of each another for added interest. Position a doo-dad appropriately to cover ends of vine.

5. Use floss or pearl cotton and a small, even utility stitch to topstitch pieces in place. Add embroidery stitches like French knots, if desired.

Quilting and Finishing

1. Mark quilting design on quilt top as desired. On quilt shown, blocks are outline-quilted, and a small squiggle is quilted in sashing. Border background is stipple-quilted with echo quilting around doo-dads.

2. Divide backing fabric into 2 equal lengths. See page 135 for instructions on making a backing.

3. Layer backing, batting, and quilt top. Baste. Quilt as desired.

4. Make 6 yards of binding. See page 139 for instructions on making and applying straight-grain binding.

Lord, give me chastity.

But not yet.

— St. Augustine

Nifty Note Cards

Make your felicitations and invitations truly notable with these personalized greeting cards. Fusible web adheres well to paper and doesn't bubble up like glue, so all your cards and coordinating envelopes will be smooth and neat.

Materials

Purchased 5" x 7" note cards with matching envelopes
Assorted fabric scraps for appliqué
Scraps of paper-backed fusible web
Pressing cloth, iron, ironing board
Black fine-tipped marker
3 (½"-diameter) buttons for each Little Lamb card
Glue stick for Little Lamb card
Pink marker for Miss Rabbit card

General Instructions

1. Trace patterns on page 40 onto paper (smooth) side of fusible web. Use paper scissors to cut out, leaving a margin of paper around each shape. *Note:* Because finished appliqué is a mirror image of printed pattern, these patterns are reversed for your convenience.

2. Place adhesive (rough) side of web on *wrong* side of appliqué fabric. Press for 5–8 seconds with a hot, dry iron. Do not overheat.

3. Let fabric cool. Use fabric scissors to cut out motif on drawn line.

4. To mark details, place cut-out piece over pattern and lightly trace lines onto right side of fabric. If you can't see pattern through fabric, use a light box or tape tracing of pattern onto a windowpane to let the sun illuminate pattern through fabric.

5. Peel off paper backing.

6. Position appliqué on right side of note card, web side down. Cover appliqué with dry press cloth. Press firmly for 10–15 seconds with hot iron. Let fabric cool.

Puffy Bird

1. On paper side of fusible web, trace bird body, beak, 2 eyes, 2 eyeballs, 2 shoes, 3 head feathers, and 4 tail feathers onto paper side of fusible web. Cut out traced pieces.

2. Press fusible web onto wrong side of appliqué fabrics.

3. Cut out fabric shapes on drawn lines. Remove paper backing.

4. Referring to photo, position body on card. Cover appliqué with dry press cloth and fuse. Add beak, eyes, and feathers in same manner.

5. Fuse shoes in place about 2½" below body.

6. For envelope, trace baby bird body, beak, head feather, and 3 tail feathers. Follow same procedure to fuse pieces onto bottom left corner of envelope.

7. Use black marker to add detail lines such as legs, wings, curlicues, eyelashes, and baby bird's legs.

Little Lambs

1. On paper side of fusible web, trace 3 lambs, 3 pairs of legs, and 3 ears onto paper side of fusible web. Cut out traced pieces.

2. Press fusible web onto wrong side of appliqué fabrics. (We used white and black felt for lamb bodies; black cotton fabrics for other pieces.)

3. Cut out fabric shapes on drawn lines. Remove paper backing.

4. Referring to photo, position 3 lamb bodies on card. Tuck legs under each body. Cover appliqués with dry press cloth and fuse. Add ears in same manner.

5. Glue or sew buttons in place between ears on each lamb.

6. Use same procedure to cut out and fuse flowers and leaves as desired at lambs' feet.

7. Use black marker to add detail lines to flowers and leaves.

8. Fuse 2 or 3 flowers onto bottom left corner of envelope.

Miss Rabbit

1. On paper side of fusible web, trace rabbit's dress, sleeves, hem, head, neck, 2 ears, 2 arms, and 2 legs onto paper side of fusible web. Cut out traced pieces.

2. Press fusible web onto wrong side of appliqué fabrics.

3. Cut out fabric shapes on drawn lines. Remove paper backing.

4. Referring to photo, position legs and hem on card. Cover appliqué with dry press cloth and fuse. Add dress, tucking sleeves, arms, and neck under dress as shown on pattern. Fuse pieces in place.

5. Position ears and head. Fuse.

6. Use black marker to draw eyes, nose, and whiskers. Referring to photo, draw dotted lines around each appliqué piece for additional detail if desired.

7. Use pink marker to fill in nose. Smudge pink marker on cheeks and ears as desired.

8. Follow same procedure to fuse ears and head onto bottom corner of envelope. We added a watermelon slice cut from print fabric. $\longrightarrow$

Adventure is worthwhile in itself. —Amelia Earhart

Miss Rabbit

Puffy Bird

Red indicates
pen/marker details.

Little Lamb

Leaf & Flower

Baby Bird

Flowerful Table Runner Patterns

Instructions begin on page 43.

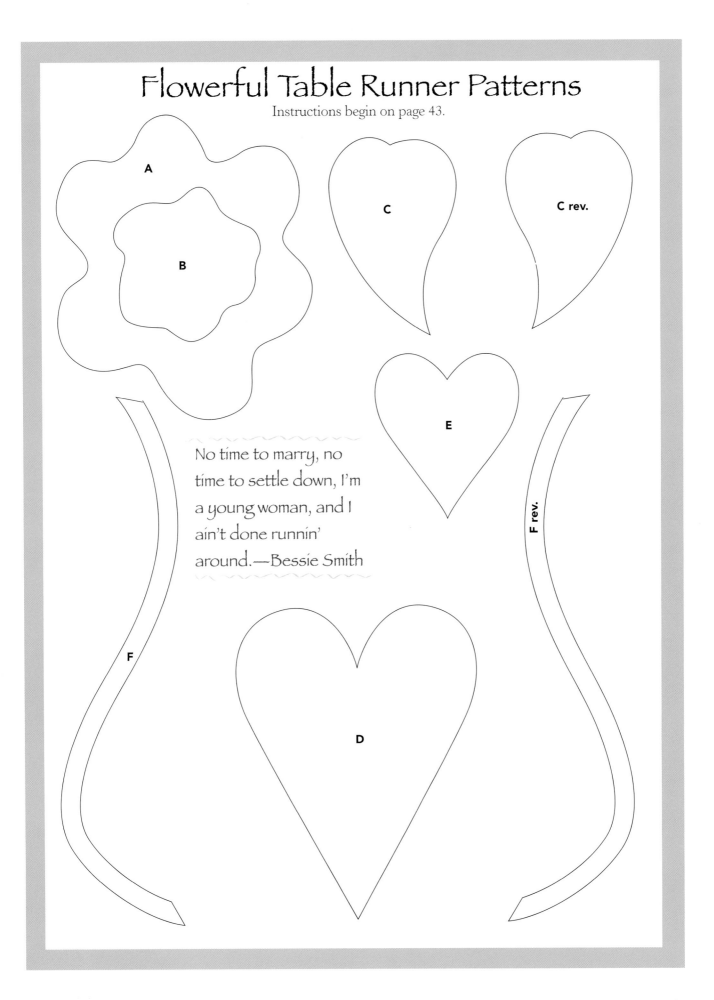

No time to marry, no time to settle down, I'm a young woman, and I ain't done runnin' around. —Bessie Smith

Flowerful Table Runner

Fusible web makes appliqué fast, easy, and fun for a variety of quick decorating projects. We started with a purchased table runner and added a wealth of hearts, leaves, and flowers for an accent piece that will do a hostess proud or make a terrific housewarming gift.

Table runner by Carol Burger of Smyrna, Georgia

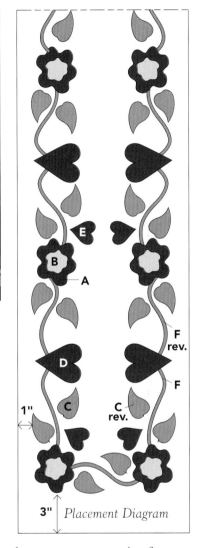

Placement Diagram

Materials

Purchased 12" x 70" table runner
(Or use 2 yards of linen to make
your own runner)
¼ yard dark green for vine
⅛ yard dark red for hearts
3½" x 7" piece *each* of 6 red prints
3" x 12" piece *each* of 4 green prints
4" square *each* of 3 yellow prints
1⅜ yards paper-backed fusible web
Pressing cloth, iron, ironing board
Tracing paper or template material

Appliqué Instructions

1. Trace patterns on page 41 onto paper (smooth) side of fusible web. Trace 12 each of A and B (flower and center), 20 each of C and C reversed (leaf), 8 D (large heart), 8 E (small heart), and 10 each of F and F reversed (vine).
2. Use paper scissors to cut drawn pieces from fusible web, leaving a margin of paper around shape.
3. Place adhesive (rough) side of each web piece on *wrong* side of appropriate appliqué fabric. Press for 5–8 seconds with a hot, dry iron. Do not overheat. Let fabric cool completely.
4. Use fabric scissors to cut out appliqué piece on drawn line.
5. Peel off paper backing.
6. Pin 2 flowers in place about 3" from corners at 1 end of runner, web side down *(Placement Diagram)*. Position pieces along sides of runner as shown, placing bottom edges of flowers and large hearts 1" from runner's edge. Tuck vine ends under hearts and flowers. When pieces are pinned on half of runner, turn it around to place pieces on second half. Adjust placement of pieces as needed.
7. When satisfied with appliqué

placement, remove pins from small section of design and cover with dry press cloth. Press firmly for 10–15 seconds with hot iron. Remove pins from next section and press in same manner. Repeat until all pieces are fused in place. Let fabrics cool.
8. Use matching or contrasting threads to run a small running stitch around each piece and through middle of each vine piece.

Coming Up Daisies

Win praise with a one-of-a-kind wearable when you say, "I made it myself." Bask in the admiration, but don't let on how easy it is to do. With fusible appliqué, you can dress up even the plainest garment in almost no time.

Shirt by Carol Burger
of Smyrna, Georgia

Materials

Purchased shirt
Scraps of white, yellow, green, and red fabrics
½ yard paper-backed fusible web
Black pearl cotton
Pressing cloth, iron, ironing board
Brown fine-tipped permanent marker

Appliqué Instructions

1. Trace patterns at right onto paper (smooth) side of fusible web. Trace as many ladybugs, stems, leaves, and flowers as you want to embellish your garment. Trace daisy petals individually.

2. Use paper scissors to cut drawn pieces from fusible web, leaving a margin of paper around shape.

3. Place adhesive (rough) side of each web piece on *wrong* side of appropriate appliqué fabric. Press for 5–8 seconds with a hot, dry iron. Do not overheat. Let fabric cool completely.

4. Use fabric scissors to cut out appliqué piece on drawn line.

5. Peel off paper backing.

6. Referring to photos, pin flowers and ladybugs in place on garment as desired. On shirt shown, bugs are hanging from flowers and leaves by their embroidered legs, but you can choose to position them in other ways.

7. When satisfied with placement, remove pins from small section of design and cover with dry press cloth. Press firmly for 10–15 seconds with hot iron. For flowers, fuse stems and leaves first; then fuse petals. Fuse yellow flower centers last. Remove pins from next section and fuse in same manner. Repeat until all pieces are fused in place. Let fabrics cool.

8. Use matching or contrasting threads to run a small running stitch through middle of each stem and around each ladybug and leaf.

Use pearl cotton to make ladybudy legs with single long stitches.

9. Use fine-tipped marker to add detail lines to daisy petals.

Note about washing: You should be able to wash the garment when fusible appliqué is complete. Even though the edges of the appliqués are not turned or finished, the fusible web prevents all but the most minute raveling. Read manufacturer's laundering tips on packaging that accompanies fusible web.

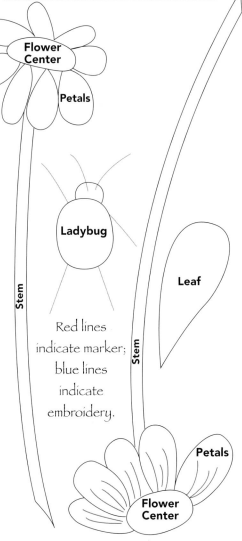

Red lines indicate marker; blue lines indicate embroidery.

Daylily

An outline of buttonhole stitch is a lovely way to dress up your appliqué. This technique isn't new—it has been around since colonial-era quilts. These days, it can be worked by machine in the wink of an eye or by hand in the traditional manner.

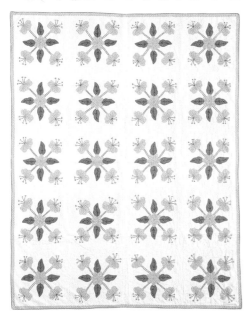

Finished Size: 70" x 87"
Blocks: 20 (17" x 17")

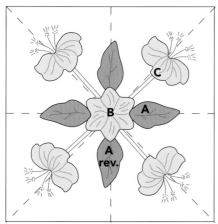

Daylily Block—Make 20.

My mother, Ida J. Warner, made 220 appliquéd pansy blocks in the 1940s. I inherited enough blocks to make 5 quilts! —Laurel Larsen, Cloverdale, California

Materials

5 yards white or muslin
2⅝ yards yellow
1½ yards green (includes binding)
5½ yards backing fabric
5 skeins orange embroidery floss
3 skeins each yellow, light green, and dark green embroidery floss
Template material
Nonpermanent marker
17" square tracing paper

Cutting

See page 126 for tips on cutting pieces for hand appliqué. Make templates of patterns A, B, and C on page 49. (Trace half of flower B; then turn template material to trace opposite half. Cut pieces in order listed to make best use of yardage.

From white, cut:
20 (17½") squares.

From yellow, cut:
2 (1½" x 93") and 2 (1½" x 76") lengthwise strips for border.
20 of Pattern B.
80 of Pattern C.

From green, cut:
30" square for binding.
40 of Pattern A.
40 of Pattern A reversed.

Making Blocks

1. Fold and crease paper square vertically, horizontally, and diagonally to make placement guides *(Diagram A)*.

2. Pattern on page 49 is ¼ of block. Place paper square over pattern, aligning guidelines on paper with red lines on pattern. Trace pattern in 4 corners of paper to make a complete pattern, including appliqué outlines and embroidery details (in blue on pattern).

3. Fold a white fabric square in half, creasing or lightly pressing folds to make placement guides for appliqué *(Diagram A)*.

4. Align fabric square with traced pattern, matching placement lines. Use a nonpermanent marker to *lightly* trace design on fabric square.

5. Use 3 strands of dark green floss to outline-stitch stems and pistils on block. (See stitch diagram, page 48.) Use 3 strands of orange floss to work pistil French knots.

6. See page 131 for tips on preparing pieces for hand appliqué. Do not turn under blunt ends of leaves that will be covered by B flower. Clip seam allowances as needed to get nice points and smooth curves.

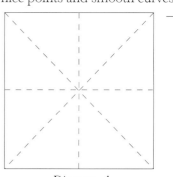

Diagram A

7. Center A, B, and C pieces over printed patterns and *lightly* trace embroidery details.

8. Referring to block diagram, pin or baste appliqué pieces onto white square. Center B flower; then align 4 A leaves with guidelines, tucking ends under B. (*Note:* Each block has 2 A leaves and 2 A reversed leaves alternating around center flower.) Position C flowers on guidelines at ends of traced stems.

9. When satisfied with placement of pieces, stitch leaves in place. Then appliqué B and C flowers. (*Note:* If you have a sewing machine that makes a buttonhole or blanket stitch, you can machine-appliqué leaves and flowers with that stitch.)

10. Follow steps 3–9 to make 20 Daylily blocks.

11. Use 3 strands of dark green floss to outline-stitch leaf veins and 3 strands of orange floss to work flower details. Use 2 strands of light green floss to work buttonhole stitch around leaves and yellow floss to stitch around flowers.

Quilt Assembly

1. Referring to photo, join blocks in 5 horizontal rows of 4 blocks each.

2. Join rows.

3. Referring to page 133, sew yellow border strips to quilt edges and miter corners.

Quilting and Finishing

1. Mark quilting design on quilt top as desired.

2. Divide backing fabric into 2 equal lengths. See page 135 for instructions on making a backing.

3. Layer backing, batting, and quilt top. Baste. Quilt as desired.

4. Make 9 yards of binding. See page 139 for instructions on making and applying binding.

Antique quilt owned by Susan Reynolds of Birmingham, Alabama

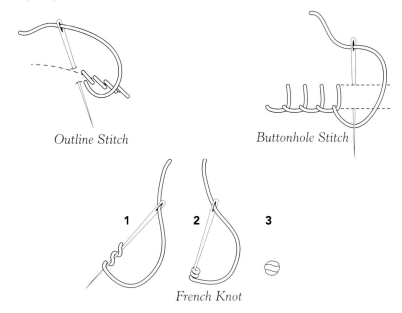

Outline Stitch

Buttonhole Stitch

French Knot

It takes great passion and great energy to do anything creative. —Agnes DeMille

A rev.

C

B

Use red lines for placement guides. Trace blue lines for embroidery details.

A

You grow up the day you have your first real laugh at yourself. —Ethel Barrymore

Between Friends

Sharing, giving, caring: these are
among the qualities that make quilting an
uplifting experience. When we work
together—for a cause or for pleasant
company—we share our passions and
sorrows, our dreams, and our bright
ideas for more and better quilts.

Friendship cannot be bought, begged, borrowed or stolen,
for it is something of no earthly good to anyone until it is
freely given away. —*Anonymous*

Rachel's Baskets,
page 56

Friendship Ribbons

Sharing fabric is an easy way to reach out and touch other quilters. These days, scrap exchanges are going on everywhere—at guild meetings and bees, between friends, and even on the Internet, people are trading squares and fat quarters. What better use for all these scraps than a quilt that's dedicated to friendship.

Finished Size: 69" x 87"
Blocks: 63 (9" x 9")

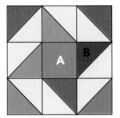

*Friendship Ribbons
Block—Make 63.*

Nobody sees a flower, really. It is so small, we haven't time, and to see takes time like to have a friend takes time.

—Georgia O'Keefe

Materials

71 (10") squares light and medium prints
71 (10") squares dark prints
99 (3½") squares dark prints
¾ yard binding fabric
5½ yards backing fabric

Making Blocks

Instructions are for quick-piecing technique. See page 130 for illustrated step-by-step instructions for stitching triangle-square grids. If you prefer a scrappier look, cut individual triangles to piece by hand or by machine.

1. On wrong side of each light square, draw a 2-square by 2-square grid of 3⅞" squares (*Diagram A*). Draw diagonal lines through each marked square as shown. Then match each light square with a dark fabric, right sides facing.

2. Stitch each grid as shown. Red lines on diagram show first path around grid, sewing into margin around grid and pivoting at corners. Blue lines show second path. When stitching is complete on both sides of diagonal lines, press.

3. Cut on all drawn lines to get 8 light/dark B triangle-squares from each grid. Stitch 71 grids to get 568 triangle-squares, 8 for each block and 64 for border units.

4. For each block, select a 3½" dark A square and 8 B triangle-squares. Arrange squares in 3 rows as shown (*Block Assembly Diagram*). Check position of triangle-squares, placing light and dark fabrics as shown.

5. When satisfied with placement, join units in each row. Press; then join rows to complete block.

6. Make 63 blocks.

No act of kindness, no matter how small, is ever wasted. —Aesop

Quilt Assembly

1. Join remaining A squares and B triangle-squares in border units (*Border Unit Diagram*). Make 32 border units as shown. You should have 4 A squares remaining. →

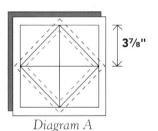

Diagram A

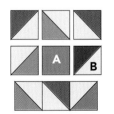

Block Assembly Diagram

Border Unit Diagram

2. Lay out blocks in 9 horizontal rows, with 7 blocks in each row *(Row Assembly Diagram)*. Arrange blocks to get a nice balance of color and value.

3. When satisfied with block placement, join blocks in each row.

4. Add border units to row ends as shown.

5. Join rows.

6. Use remaining border units and squares to make 2 border rows as shown. Referring to photo, sew 1 border row to top edge of quilt. Turn second border row upside down and sew it to bottom edge.

Quilting and Finishing

1. Mark quilting design on quilt top as desired. Quilt shown is outline-quilted.

2. Divide backing into 2 equal lengths. See page 135 for instructions on making a backing.

3. Layer backing, batting, and quilt top. Baste. Quilt as desired.

4. Make 9 yards of binding. See page 139 for instructions on making and applying binding.

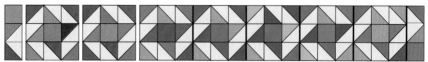

Block Row—Make 9.

Border Row—Make 2.

Row Assembly Diagram

Quilt by Kitty Sorgen of Newbury Park, California,
for Jill and Andy Urbach of Barrington, Illinois; hand-quilted by Jean Byrd.

Quilt Project Brings Helping Hands to Tornado Victims

States are represented by blocks like this bunch of chili peppers from Arizona (top) and a New Hampshire moose.

Teacher Kay Johnson displays 50-state quilt made by 5th graders, with help from quilters nationwide and local volunteers.

A tornado carried Dorothy to the Land of Oz. In April, 1998, a tornado and a quilt took some Alabama children to Alaska. And New Hampshire. And every other state in the Union.

The project actually began before the winds blew. Fifth-grade teacher Kay Johnson wanted to enhance motor skills for students at Concord Elementary in Bessemer, a suburb of Birmingham. A newcomer to quilting, Kay decided to combine quiltmaking and geography.

All it took was a note on an Internet bulletin board. Kay asked quilters to contribute 6"-square quilt blocks representing their states, while assigning each student a state to research. As blocks came pouring in, students corresponded with the donors to learn more about distant places.

Pinson, Alabama, quilter Kathy English assembled the quilt top for the class. With the help of other volunteers, all 330 children in the school took turns putting in quilting stitches.

Then the tornado came. The winds that roared through the April night destroyed the homes of several Concord students. As the news hit the airwaves, quilters everywhere sprang to action.

Kay's Internet buddies lost no time swamping her with e-mail. "Are you all right?" came from across the country and even from overseas. Quilters sent donations of cash and clothing.

Then came the quilts. On the Internet, Kay wrote, "I wish I had a quilt to wrap around each of these kids, like arms to wrap around them." The response was sure and swift— 48 quilts came from caring people around the world, one for every child and teacher at Concord who lost a home to the storm.

Mark Roper learned about Alaska from the quilter who made a timber wolf block to represent her state.

The children finished their 50-state quilt with renewed enthusiasm. They learned about quiltmaking and the U.S. states. And the children of Concord Elementary learned about the kindness of strangers.

Rachel's Baskets

Finding a place in your heart for a little girl is the easiest thing in the world.

Second easiest—quick-piecing a quilt for her. Kitty Sorgen created this sweet pastel patchwork for her granddaughter. Little Rachel already knows that a quilt is a gift of love.

Finished Size: 71" x 85"

Blocks: 17 (10" x 10") Basket blocks
32 (10" x 10") Log Cabin blocks

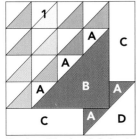

Basket Block—Make 17.

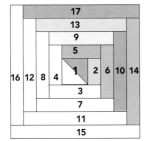

Log Cabin Block—Make 32.

Materials

4½ yards white or muslin
17 (¼-yard) pieces pastel prints
¾ yard binding fabric
5¼ yards backing fabric

Cutting

Instructions are for quick-piecing technique. See page 130 for illustrated step-by-step instructions for stitching triangle-square grids. (If you prefer a scrappier look, cut individual triangles to piece by hand or by machine.) Cut pieces in order listed to get most efficient use of yardage.

From white, cut:

6 (15½") squares. Cut each square in quarters diagonally to get 22 setting triangles (and 2 extra).

4 (8"-wide) cross-grain strips. From these, cut 16 (8" x 10½") pieces for triangle-square grids. Use waste from previous cut to get 1 more 8" x 10½" piece for a total of 17 pieces.

40 (1½"-wide) cross-grain strips for Log Cabin blocks.

2 (6½"-wide) cross-grain strips. From these, cut 34 (2½" x 6½") C pieces.

9 (4⅞") squares. Cut each square in half diagonally to get 17 D triangles (and 1 extra).

26 (2⅞") squares. Cut each square in half diagonally to get 51 A triangles (and 1 extra).

In spite of everything, I still believe that people are really good at heart. —Anne Frank

From each pastel print, cut:

1 (8" x 10½") piece for triangle-square grids.

1 (7") square. Cut square in half diagonally to get 1 B triangle. From remaining triangle, cut 1 (2⅞") square. Cut this square in half diagonally to get 2 A triangles.

6 (1½" x 25½") strips for Log Cabin blocks.

Basket Blocks

1. On wrong side of each white square, draw a 2-square by 3-square grid of 2⅞" squares *(Diagram A)*. Draw diagonal lines through each marked square as shown. Then match each light square with a dark fabric, right sides facing.

2. Stitch each grid as shown. Red lines on diagram show first path around grid, sewing into margin around grid and pivoting at corners. Blue lines show second path. When stitching is complete on both sides of diagonal lines, press.

3. Cut on all lines to get 12 triangle-squares from each grid. Stitch 17 grids to get 204 triangle-squares, 10 for each Basket block, 1 for each Log Cabin block, and 2 extra.

→

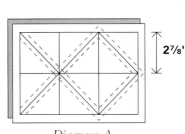

Diagram A

4. For each Basket block, select 10 triangle-squares and 3 white A triangles. Arrange squares and triangles in 4 horizontal rows as shown *(Diagram B)*. Check position of triangle-squares, placing white and print fabrics as shown. When satisfied with placement, join units in each row. Press; then join rows.

5. To complete block, select 1 B triangle and 2 matching A triangles, as well as 2 Cs and 1 D.

6. Sew B triangle to diagonal edge of triangle-square unit *(Basket Block Assembly Diagram)*. Press seam allowance toward B.

7. Join an A triangle to 1 end of each C piece. Be sure to position triangles as shown to get 2 mirror-image units. Press seam allowances toward C.

8. Sew A/C units to block sides as shown. Press seam allowances toward A/C units.

9. Add D triangle to complete block. Press seam allowance toward D.

10. Make 17 Basket blocks.

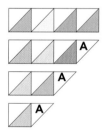

Diagram B

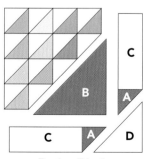

Basket Block Assembly Diagram

Log Cabin Blocks

It is not necessary to precut individual pieces for logs with this stitch-and-flip method.

1. For each block, start with 1 triangle-square. Select a print strip for first log. With right sides facing, match strip to print side of triangle-square as shown *(Diagram C)*. Be sure triangle-square is positioned correctly; then stitch. Trim log even with bottom of square. Press seam allowance toward log.

2. Position sewn unit with new log at top. Match a white strip to side of unit as shown *(Diagram D)*, right sides facing, and stitch. Trim white strip even with center square. Press seam allowance toward new log.

3. Turn block to position new log at top. With right sides facing, match

white strip to right edge and stitch *(Diagram E)*. Trim log even with block as before and press seam allowance toward new log.

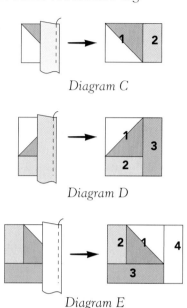

Diagram C

Diagram D

Diagram E

Quilt by Kitty Sorgen of Newbury Park, California, for her granddaughter Rachel Hildreth; machine-quilted by Marilyn Peterson.

4. Turn unit so newest log is at top. With right sides facing, match a new print strip to right edge of block and stitch *(Diagram F)*. Trim log even with block and press.

5. Continue adding logs in this manner until you have 4 logs on each side of center triangle-square *(Block Diagram)*. Always press seam allowances toward newest log; then rotate unit to put new log at top before you add next strip.

6. Make 32 Log Cabin blocks.

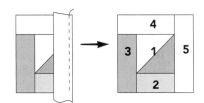

Diagram F

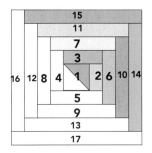

Log Cabin Block Diagram

Quilt Assembly

1. Lay out Basket blocks in diagonal rows as shown *(Quilt Assembly Diagram)*. Arrange blocks to get a nice balance of color and value.

2. Add Log Cabin blocks and setting triangles to row ends as shown. Double-check to be sure each Log Cabin block is positioned correctly.

3. When satisfied with placement, join blocks and setting triangles in each row. You will have 4 setting triangles left over for corner units.

4. Join rows.

5. Join remaining setting triangles to make 2 corner units as shown. Sew corners in place.

Quilting and Finishing

1. See page 126 for tips on cutting appliqué pieces. Make templates of flower, flower center, and leaf patterns on page 58. From scraps, cut 4 each of flower and flower center, and 8 leaves.

2. Referring to photo, center flowers over diagonal seam between Log Cabin blocks at each corner. Pin flowers and flower centers in place. Tuck leaves under flowers. When satisfied with placement, appliqué pieces in place.

3. Mark quilting design on quilt top as desired. Quilt shown is machine-quilted with a large feather pattern over Log Cabin border.

4. Cut backing fabric into 2 equal lengths. See page 135 for instructions on piecing a backing.

5. Layer backing, batting, and quilt top. Baste. Quilt as desired.

6. Make 9 yards of binding. See page 139 for instructions on making and applying binding.

Quilt Assembly Diagram

Rachel helps her grandmother, Kitty Sorgen, piece the backing for her quilt. *Rachel's Baskets* will travel with Kitty when she makes her annual trip to Norway to teach and to visit relatives.

Chains of Love

The interlocking chains of this Garden Maze variation are like the threads of the five lives who created it. Flying Geese and Goslings of Omaha, Nebraska, are five women (and their children) entering a second decade of quilting together. Like the patches of the quilt, it takes a lot of piecing to keep friendships together across time and distance. This group combines friends and family with quilt plans for the future. (See box, page 62.)

Finished Size: 93½" x 104½"
Blocks: 161 (5½" x 5½") Block 1
90 (5½" x 5½") Block 2

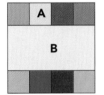

Block 1—Make 161.

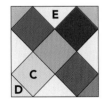

Block 2—Make 90.

If thine enemy be hungry, give him bread to eat. And if he be thirsty, give him water to drink. —Proverbs 25:21

Materials

5 yards muslin
24 assorted fat quarters
1 yard binding fabric
3⅛ yards 108"-wide backing fabric

Cutting

Cutting instructions are for quick-piecing technique. To make efficient use of yardage, cut pieces in order listed. Cut all strips cross-grain.

From muslin, cut:

23 (6"-wide) strips. From these, cut 72 (6") setting squares and 161 (3¼" x 6") B pieces.

9 (4"-wide) strips. From these, cut 90 (4") squares. Cut each square in quarters diagonally to get 360 E triangles.

From each fat quarter, cut:

6 (1⅞" x 18") strips for Strip Set 1.

1 (2¼" x 18") strip. Cut 8 (2¼") squares from each strip. Cut each square in half diagonally to get 360 D triangles (and 24 extra).

3 (2½" x 18") for Strip Set 2.

Block 1

1. For Strip Set 1, join any 4 (1⅞"-wide) strips (*Strip Set 1 Diagram*). Make 36 strip sets, varying fabric combinations as much as possible.

1⅞"

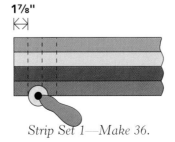

Strip Set 1—Make 36.

Press. If you prefer traditional piecing, cut 1,288 (1⅞") A squares from strips and piece as shown.

2. Rotary-cut 9 (1⅞"-wide) segments from each strip set to get a total of 322 segments (and 2 extra).

3. To assemble block, sew segments to long sides of each B piece. Press seam allowances toward B.

4. Make 161 of Block 1.

Block 2

1. For Strip Set 2, join 3 (2½"-wide) strips (*Strip Set 2 Diagram*). Stitch seams with a generous ¼" seam allowance. Make 13 strip sets, varying fabric combinations. Press seam allowances away from center strip.

2. Cut 7 (2½"-wide) segments from each strip set to get a total of 90 segments, 1 for each block.

3. Sew D triangles to ends of each segment (*Diagram A*). Press seam allowances away from squares.

$\longrightarrow$

2½"

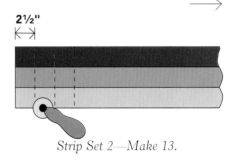

Strip Set 2—Make 13.

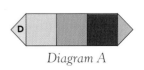

Diagram A

4. From remaining 2½"-wide strips, cut 180 (2½") C squares.

5. Sew E triangles to opposite sides of each C square *(Diagram B)*. Press seam allowances toward Cs. Add a D triangle to each unit as shown. Make 180 C/D/E corner units, 2 for each block.

6. Sew corner units to both sides of center segment *(Block 2 Assembly Diagram)*.

7. Make 90 of Block 2.

Quilt Assembly

Refer to *Row Assembly Diagram* throughout.

1. For Row 1, lay out 10 of Block 2 and 9 of Block 1, alternating blocks as shown. Lay out 9 of Row 1.

2. For Row 2, alternate 10 of Block 1 with 9 plain setting squares as shown. Lay out 8 of Row 2.

3. When blocks are placed as desired, join blocks in each row. Press seam allowances toward Block 1 in all rows.

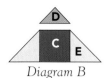

Diagram B

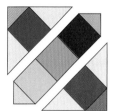

Block 2 Assembly Diagram

4. Referring to photo, join rows, alternating rows 1 and 2 as shown.

Quilting and Finishing

1. Mark quilting design on quilt top as desired. Quilt shown is outline-quilted. For setting squares, purchase or make a stencil of a design 4½" to 5" square or round.

2. Layer backing, batting, and quilt top. Baste. Quilt as desired.

3. Make 11¼ yards of binding. See page 139 for instructions on making and applying binding.

*Row 1—
Make 9.*

*Row 2—
Make 8.*

Row Assembly Diagram

Wedding Bells Herald Quilts for Goslings

As the children of Flying Geese and Goslings leave home, each young adult will have a quilt with which to feather a new nest.

When the Omaha group first met, the five members were young mothers with babies who included their children in weekly get-togethers. More than a decade later, the children are growing up, so the Geese are hatching a plan to make a wedding quilt for each child—an ambitious undertaking since, among them, the group has 17 children.

Chains of Love is the second wedding quilt the group completed, made for the marriage of Barbara Rennard's daughter, Emily. The first was a Wedding Ring quilt, made for Barbara's daughter, Rachael.

While the Geese wait for the next engagement to be announced, member Sandy Harris quilts long-distance from Virginia—"but is with us in spirit." Quilts are planned for her four children as well as those of Claudia Swee, Deb Hickman, and Jayne Schlosser.

Many of the children are still teens, but with another 15 offspring to provide quilts for, the Flying Geese have quite a lot of quilting to do.

Special Ruler Available
The Flying Geese and Goslings made this quilt from a pattern published by Julie Larsen of Prairie Star Patterns. Julie's booklet includes a special ruler and a method that eliminates cutting any triangles. For more information about this alternate Chains of Love technique, contact Prairie Star Patterns, 4132 Main Street, Elk Horn, IA 51531 or call (712) 764-7012.

Every day, do something nice and try not to get caught. —Anonymous

Quilt by Deb Hickman, Barbara Rennard, Jayne Schlosser, and Claudia Swee of Omaha, Nebraska, and Sandy Harris of Springfield, Virginia, from a design by Prairie Star Patterns.

Buttercream Blues

The block swap is a popular way to quilt with and for friends. If your group is making a quilt for a charity raffle, giving blocks to a friend, or trading blocks with each other, try this scrappy Sister's Choice quilt. After all, we're all sisters in quilting (and a few brothers, too). Choose a theme fabric and let it set the color scheme.

Finished Size: 67" x 88¼"
Blocks: 35 (7½" x 7½")

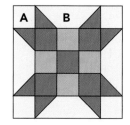

Sister's Choice Block—Make 35.

Materials

2⅛ yards theme print
5 (¼-yard) pieces yellow prints
35 (2"-wide) strips light prints*
17 (2"-wide) strips medium prints*
35 (2"-wide) strips dark prints*
¾ yard binding fabric
5½ yards backing fabric
* All strips cross-grain, 44" long.

Cutting

Instructions are for rotary cutting. To make efficient use of yardage, cut pieces in order listed.

From theme print, cut:

4 (7¼" x 76") lengthwise strips for border.

5 (12") squares. Cut each square in quarters diagonally to get 20 setting triangles.

2 (6⅛") squares. Cut each square in half diagonally to get 4 corner triangles.

Add scraps to fabrics for blocks, if desired.

From yellow prints, cut:

24 (8") setting squares.

Making Blocks

See page 128 for illustrated step-by-step instructions for diagonal-corner technique.

1. For each block, select 1 each of a light and a dark fabric strip, as well as ½ of a medium strip.

2. From light strip, cut 4 (2") A squares and 4 (2" x 5") B rectangles.

3. From medium strip, cut 4 (2") A squares.

4. From dark strip, cut 13 (2") A squares.

5. For center nine-patch, select 5 dark and 4 medium squares. Join squares in 3 rows of 3 squares each *(Diagram A)*. Press seam allowances toward medium squares. Join rows to make nine-patch.

6. Use diagonal-corner technique to sew remaining dark squares to both ends of each B rectangle *(Diagram B)*. Make 4 units as shown.

7. Arrange completed units in 3 horizontal rows *(Block Assembly Diagram)*. Join units in each row; press seam allowances away from B units. Join rows to complete block.

8. Make 35 Sister's Choice blocks.

→

It is better to light a candle than to curse the dark- ness. —Eleanor Roosevelt

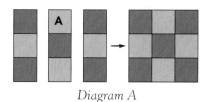

Diagram A

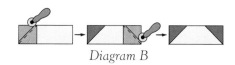

Diagram B

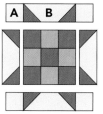

Block Assembly Diagram

Quilt Assembly

1. Lay out blocks and setting squares in 11 diagonal rows *(Quilt Assembly Diagram)*. Arrange blocks and squares to get a pleasing balance of color and value. Add setting triangles and/or corner triangles to ends of each row as shown.

2. When satisfied with placement, join units in each row. Press seam allowances toward setting pieces.

3. Join rows.

Border

1. Referring to page 132, measure quilt from top to bottom through middle of quilt. Trim 2 border strips to match length. Sew these to quilt sides. Press seam allowances toward borders.

2. Measure quilt from side to side through middle of quilt. Trim remaining borders to match quilt width. Sew trimmed borders to top and bottom edges. Press seam allowances toward borders.

Quilting and Finishing

1. Mark quilting design on quilt top as desired. Quilt shown is outline-quilted with a heart design quilted in each setting square. Lines of cross-hatching in setting triangles and borders are spaced 1½" apart.

2. Divide backing into 2 equal lengths. See page 135 for instructions on making a backing.

3. Layer backing, batting, and quilt top. Baste. Quilt as desired.

4. Make 9 yards of binding. See page 139 for instructions on making and applying binding.

Quilt Assembly Diagram

If I am not for myself, who will be for me? But if I am for myself alone, what am I?
— Hillel (Jewish philosopher, 30 B.C.–A.D. 10)

Quilt by Kitty Sorgen of Newbury Park, California; hand-quilted by Debra Duncan.

Purely for the Pleasure

For many, quiltmaking is all the more worthwhile when it's a challenge. These are quilts for those who raise the bar ever higher in a quest for the exceptional, no matter how intricate or time-consuming. When you find peace in quiet time alone and the soothing rhythm of the needle, you know the pleasure of fine piecework and fancy quilting.

If of thy material goods thou art bereft,
And from thy slender store
Two loaves alone to thee are left,
Sell one, and with the dole
Buy hyacinths to feed thy soul.
— Moslih Eddin Saad, 12th-century Persian poet

Princess Feathers,
page 90

Baby Baskets

This lightweight quilt was made in the late 1800s, probably in Indiana or Kentucky, by someone who had a nice collection of plaid fabrics. The red checked theme fabric is an unusual choice for the period, as is the vertical set. Combine your favorite scraps with an exciting theme fabric to make a contemporary version of this sweet antique.

Finished Size: 67" x 77"
Blocks: 77 (7" x 7")

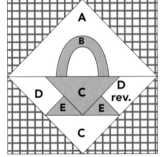

Baby Basket Block—Make 77.

Materials

3½ yards muslin (includes binding)
3 yards red check*
13 (⅛-yard) pieces or scraps
2 yards 90"-wide backing fabric
* In the original quilt, block corners are cut on the bias. This requires more yardage and adds the problem of working with bias edges on the outside of the blocks. Yardage given is for block corners cut on the straight of the grain.

Cutting

Instructions are for both traditional and rotary cutting. Make a template of patterns B and D on page 73, referring to page 126 for tips on making templates for piecing and for appliqué. Other pieces can be rotary cut.

From muslin, cut:

12 (1½" x 80") lengthwise strips for sashing.

39 (5⅞") squares. Cut each square in half diagonally to get 77 A triangles (and 1 extra).

39 (3½") squares. Cut each square in half diagonally to get 77 C triangles (and 1 extra).

77 of Pattern D.

77 of Pattern D reversed.

From red check, cut:

6 (1½" x 80") lengthwise strips for sashing.

154 (4½") squares. Cut each square in half diagonally to get 308 corner triangles.

From scraps, cut:

39 (3½") squares. Cut each square in half diagonally to get 77 C triangles (and 1 extra).

77 (2⅛") squares. Cut each square in half diagonally to get 154 E triangles.

77 of Pattern B. Add seam allowance around template when cutting Bs.

Making Blocks

1. For each block, select 1 each of muslin A, C, D, and D reversed. From scraps, select 2 E triangles and 1 each of B handle and C triangle. Scrap fabrics can be uniform in each block like the quilt shown or you can mix up scraps as desired.

2. Turn under seam allowance on B curves. Leave seam allowance unturned at bottom straight ends.

3. Fold A triangle in half and crease to mark center. Fold B in same manner. Center B on A triangle, matching centers and aligning straight edges (*Block Assembly Diagram*). Appliqué B onto A. Press.

4. Stitch E triangles onto straight ends of D and D reversed. Press seam allowances toward triangles.

5. Sew D/E units onto short legs of C scrap triangle as shown. Press seam allowances toward C.

6. Join muslin C triangle to bottom of basket unit as shown. Press seam allowance toward C triangle.   ⟶

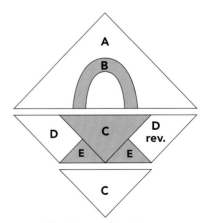

Block Assembly Diagram

7. Join 2 halves of basket. Press seam allowance toward A triangle.
8. Add a check corner triangle to 2 opposite sides of block. Press seam allowances toward corner triangles. Then add triangles to remaining opposite corners to complete block.
9. Make 77 basket blocks.

Quilt Assembly

1. Lay out blocks in 7 vertical rows, with 11 blocks in each row. Arrange blocks as desired to achieve a nice balance of color and value.
2. When satisfied with placement, join blocks in each row.
3. Stitch each check sashing strip between 2 muslin strips. Make 6 muslin/check/muslin sashings. Press seams toward check.
4. Referring to photo, join block rows with sashing strips between each row. (Sashing may be longer than block rows). Press seam allowances toward sashing.
5. Trim sashing even with block rows.

Quilting and Finishing

1. Mark quilting design on quilt top as desired. Quilt shown is outline-quilted.
2. Layer backing, batting, and quilt top. Baste. Quilt as desired.
3. Make 8¼ yards of binding from remaining muslin. See page 139 for instructions on making and applying binding.

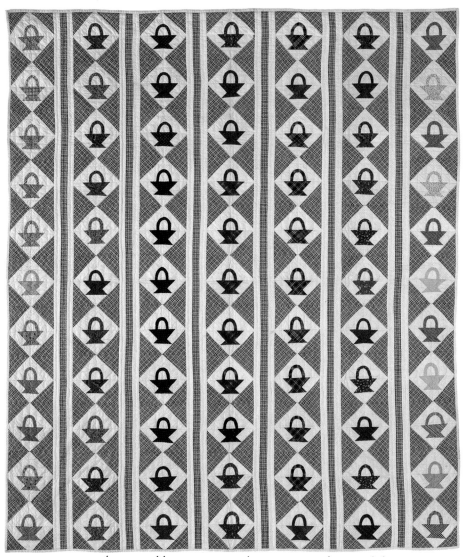

Antique quilt owned by Patricia Wilens, Birmingham, Alabama

From birth to age 18, a girl needs good parents. From 18 to 35, she needs good looks. From 35 to 55, a woman needs personality. And from 55 on, the old lady needs cash. —Kathleen Norris, American author, 1880–1966 (also attributed to singer Sophie Tucker)

A

B

C

D

E

Tree of Life

Colonial-era quilters often set blocks pointing to the quilt's middle rather than marching along in uniform position. This antique set, reproduction fabrics, and an abundance of triangles lift this traditional design to new heights. Sawtooth borders frame a pieced border reminiscent of a Delectable Mountains design.

Finished Size: 75" x 75"
Blocks: 22 (10" x 10")

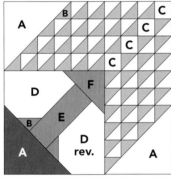

Tree of Life Block—Make 22.

Materials

7¾ yards cream mini-print or muslin
6 (¼-yard) pieces or scraps for tree trunks, leaf appliqués
25 (¼-yard) pieces or scraps for triangles
11 (4⅞") squares for ground
⅞ yard binding fabric
5 yards backing fabric

Cutting

Instructions are for quick-piecing technique. If you prefer, you can cut individual triangles for hand piecing. To make efficient use of yardage, cut pieces in order listed (large pieces first; then small pieces from leftovers). See this page for Leaf Pattern and page 79 for Pattern D. Other pieces are rotary-cut.

From cream print, cut:

4 (15½") squares. Cut each square in quarters diagonally to get 12 G setting triangles.
2 (13½") squares. Cut each square in half diagonally to get 4 Z triangles.
5 (12½") squares. Cut each square in quarters diagonally to get 20 X triangles.
4 (11¼") squares. Cut each square in quarters diagonally to get 16 Y triangles.
3 (10½") setting squares.
2 (8") squares. Cut each square in half diagonally to get 4 H triangles.
43 (7") squares for sawtooth border triangle-square grids.
74 (6" x 9½") for block and mountain border triangle-square grids.
22 (4⅞") squares. Cut each square in half diagonally to get 44 A triangles.
22 of Pattern D and 22 of Pattern D reversed.
3 (1½"-wide) cross-grain strips. From these, cut 88 (1½") C squares.

From *each* trunk fabric, cut:

2 of Leaf Pattern. (Cut 4 leaves with long stems and 8 with shorter stems as indicated on pattern.)
2 (4" x 10") rectangles. Set aside 1 rectangle. From remaining rectangle, cut 2 (2" x 4⅜") E pieces, 1 (3⅜") square, and 2 (1⅞") squares. Cut squares in half diagonally to get 2 F triangles and 4 B triangles. Sort 22 sets of matching trunk pieces, 1 for each block.

From scraps, cut:

43 (7") squares for sawtooth border triangle-square grids.
74 (6" x 9½") for block and mountain border triangle-square grids.
98 (1⅞") squares. Cut each square in half to get 196 B triangles.

Making Blocks

See page 130 for illustrated step-by-step instructions for sewing triangle-square grids. Refer to block diagram throughout.

1. On wrong side of each 6" x 9½" cream rectangle, draw a 2-square by 4-square grid of 1⅞" squares *(Diagram A)*. Draw diagonal lines through each marked square as shown. Then match each cream rectangle with a scrap rectangle of the same size, right sides facing.

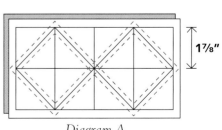

Diagram A

Cut here for short-stemmed leaves.

Leaf

2. Stitch each grid as shown. Red lines on diagram show first path around grid, sewing into margin and pivoting at corners. Blue lines show second path. When stitching is complete on both sides of diagonal lines, press. Cut on drawn lines to get 16 scrap/cream triangle-squares from each grid. Stitch 55 grids to get 880 triangle-squares, 40 for each block. (Set aside 19 grids for mountain border.)

3. Cut each ground triangle in half diagonally to get 22 A triangles, 1 for each block.

4. For each block, select 40 triangle-squares, 8 scrap B triangles, 4 C squares, 2 cream A triangles, 1 set of trunk pieces (2 Bs, 1 E, 1F), 1 ground A triangle, and 1 each of D and D reversed.

5. For Section 1, arrange triangle-squares, C squares, and B triangles in 4 horizontal rows as shown *(Block Assembly Diagram)*. Position triangle-squares as shown, changing position on opposite sides of C squares. When satisfied with placement, join units in each row. Press; then join rows. Add cream A triangle as shown to complete Section 1. Press seam allowance toward A.

6. For Section 2, arrange triangle-squares and B triangles in rows as shown. Join units in each row.

Press; then join rows. Add cream A triangle as shown to complete Section 2. Press seam allowance toward A.

7. For trunk section, sew trunk B triangles to short edges of D and D reverse pieces as shown. Press seam allowances toward Ds.

8. Sew D/B units to opposite sides of E. Press seams toward E.

9. Join A and F triangles to trunk unit corners to complete trunk section. Press seams toward triangles.

10. Join sections 2 and 3. Press. Join Section 1 to complete block.

11. Make 22 Tree of Life blocks.

Quilt Assembly

1. Lay out blocks, setting squares, G setting triangles, and H corner triangles in 7 diagonal rows *(Quilt Assembly Diagram)*. Position tree blocks as shown or as desired.

2. When satisfied with block placement, join blocks and triangles in each row.

3. Join rows. Add remaining corner triangles to first and last rows as shown. Press seams. Assembled quilt top should measure approximately 57" square.

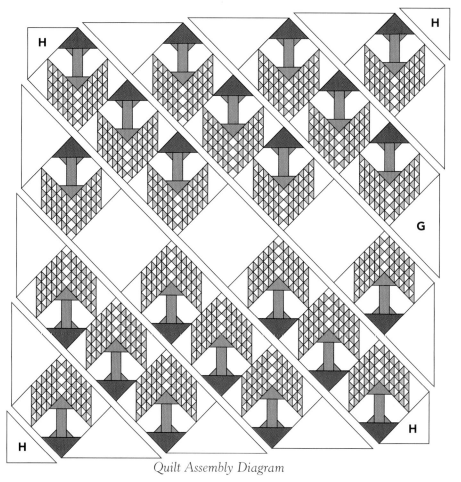

Quilt Assembly Diagram

Real joy comes not from ease or riches or from the praise of men; but from doing something worthwhile.
—Wilfred Grenfell

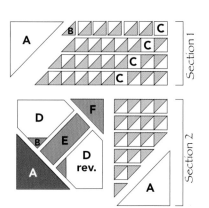

Block Assembly Diagram

Sawtooth Border

1. On wrong side of each 7" cream square, draw a 2-square by 2-square grid of 2⅜" squares *(Diagram B)*. Draw diagonal lines through each square as shown. Then match each cream square with a scrap square of the same size, right sides facing.

2. Stitch each grid as shown. Red lines on diagram show first path around grid, sewing into margin around grid and pivoting at corners. Blue lines show second path. When stitching is complete on both sides of diagonal lines, press. Cut on drawn lines to get 8 scrap/cream triangle-squares from each grid. Stitch 19 grids to get 148 triangle-squares for first border. (Set aside remaining grids and triangle-squares for outer border.)

3. Referring to photo, join 37 triangle-squares in a row for each quilt side.

4. Join a triangle-square row to opposite sides of quilt, easing to fit as needed.

5. From scrap, cut 4 (1⅞") squares for border corners. Sew a square onto each end of both remaining rows. Sew rows to remaining quilt sides, easing to fit as needed.

Mountain Border

1. Mark and stitch remaining 6" x 9½" triangle-square grids (see Making Blocks, Step 1, and *Diagram A*). Cut out 304 triangle-squares.

2. Join 7 triangle-squares in a row *(Diagram C)*. Sew this strip to 1 short leg of a Y triangle. Press seam allowance toward Y.

3. Join 8 more triangle-squares in a row, turning first triangle-square in different direction as shown. Add a B triangle at row end. Sew this row to remaining short leg of Y triangle. Press seam allowance toward Y.

Quilt by Gerry Sweem of Reseda, California

4. Sew an X triangle to top edge of Y unit as shown.

5. Make 16 X/Y units.

6. Join 4 X/Y units for each border, sewing left edge of X triangle to right edge of preceding Y unit *(Diagram D)*. Add 1 more X triangle to right end of each row as shown.

7. Sew 1 assembled border to each quilt side. →

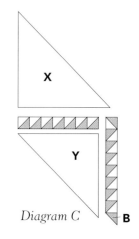

Diagram C

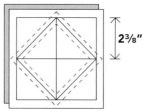

Diagram B

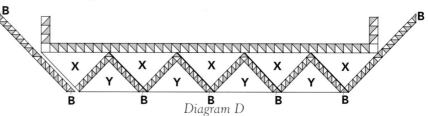

Diagram D

**½ Feathered
Wreath
Quilting Pattern**

8. To finish corners, join remaining triangle-squares and B triangles in 4 rows as shown (left corner, *Diagram D*), sewing 16 triangle-squares and 2 Bs in each row. Stitch rows across corners as shown.

9. Stitch Z triangles onto each corner to square up quilt top.

10. Use remaining 7"-square grids to stitch and cut out 196 triangle-squares for outer sawtooth border.

11. Make 2 rows of 48 triangle-squares each. Stitch rows to 2 opposite sides of quilt. Join remaining triangle-squares in 2 rows of 50 and sew these to remaining quilt sides.

Quilting and Finishing

1. Referring to photo, appliqué leaves on Z triangles. Center 1 long-stemmed leaf at each corner; then overlap a short-stemmed leaf on each side as shown.

2. Mark quilting design on quilt top as desired. On quilt shown, triangle-squares are outline-quilted. Patterns for feather wreaths quilted in setting pieces and mountain border triangles are at left and on page 79. See page 134 for tips on making your own quilting stencils.

3. Divide backing into 2 equal lengths. See page 135 for instructions on making a backing.

4. Layer backing, batting, and quilt top. Baste. Quilt as desired.

5. Make 8½ yards of binding. See page 139 for instructions on making and applying binding.

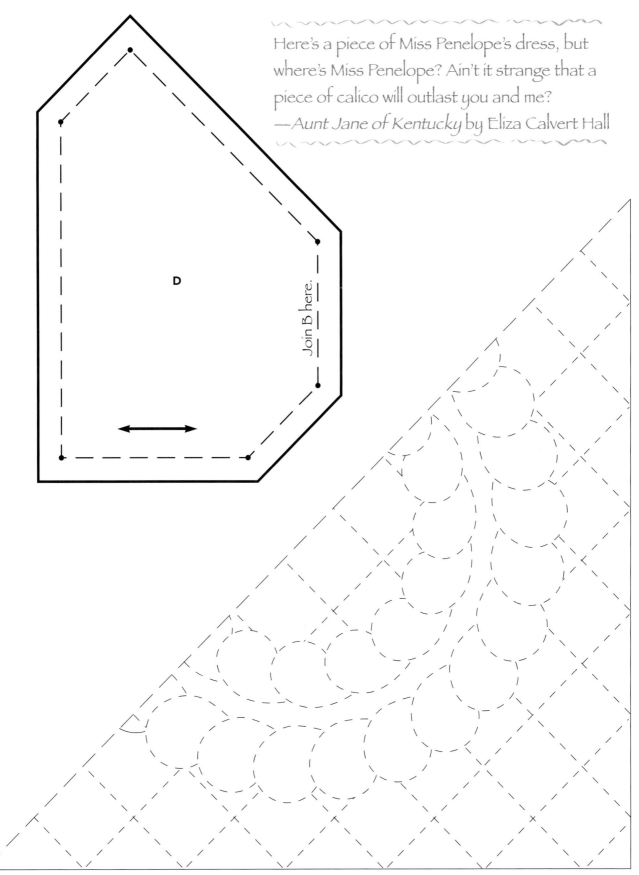

D

Join B here.

Here's a piece of Miss Penelope's dress, but where's Miss Penelope? Ain't it strange that a piece of calico will outlast you and me?
—*Aunt Jane of Kentucky* by Eliza Calvert Hall

Border Triangle Quilting Pattern

Reviving Traditions

Depression-era quilters made many colorful scrap quilts using a foundation-piecing technique called "string" piecing—because every little string of fabric can be useful. Wanda Kertis revisits this tradition with a cheerful variation of an Indian Hatchets block. Enhanced with an exquisite feather-quilted border and a scalloped edge, this design combines opportunities for care-free piecing and lovely handwork.

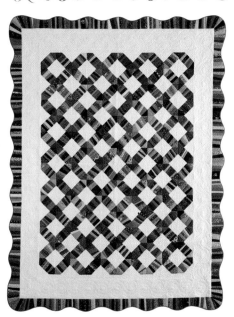

Finished Size: 74½" x 95½"
Blocks: 35 (10½" x 10½")

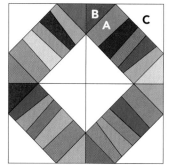

Paths to Piece Block—Make 35.

The brain is a wonderful organ. It starts working the moment you get up in the morning and doesn't stop until you get into the office.
—Robert Frost

Materials

3⅝ yards white
1⅜ yards muslin or white for border foundation piecing
45 (3⅜"-wide) scrap strips (blocks)
16 (4½"-wide) scrap strips (border)
⅞ yard binding fabric
5⅝ yards backing fabric

Cutting

Instructions are for rotary cutting. To make efficient use of yardage, cut pieces in order listed.

From white, cut:

2 (7¼" x 96") and 2 (7¼" x 75") lengthwise strips for middle border.

140 (4⅛") squares. Cut each square in half diagonally to get 280 C triangles.

From 3⅜"-wide strips, cut:

140 (2⅞") squares. Cut each square in half diagonally to get 280 B triangles.

Approximately 800 (3⅜"-long) pieces, ranging from 1" wide to 2" wide. Precise number needed will vary with random size of strips, or strings. You need 5 or 6 strings for each quarter-block.

Making Blocks

This block has many names; we like Paths to Piece. Refer to block diagram throughout. Each block has 4 units, all made the same way but using different scrap fabrics.

1. For first quarter-unit, piece 5 or 6 strings in a row to make a unit 5" long *(Diagram A)*. Seams do not have to be straight (isn't that a nice change of pace?)—in fact, the more varied the piece, the more interesting the finished quilt. Press.

2. Sew B triangles to ends of pieced strip *(Diagram B)*. Press seam allowances away from triangles.

3. Sew white C triangles to opposite sides of pieced strip *(Diagram C)*. Center triangle on strip, leaving seam allowance "ears" extending evenly at both sides. (These will be trimmed later.) Press seam allowances toward triangles.

4. Make 140 quarter-units in this manner. →

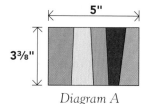

Diagram A

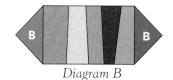

Diagram B

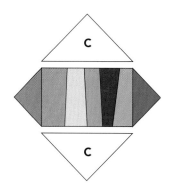

Diagram C

5. Select 4 quarter-units for each block. Lay out blocks as shown *(Block Assembly Diagram)*, turning white triangles to center and outer corners of block. Join units in 2 rows as shown; press seam allowances in opposite directions. Then join rows to complete block.

6. Make 35 Paths to Piece blocks.

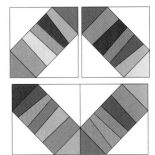

Block Assembly Diagram

Quilt Assembly

1. Referring to photo, lay out blocks in 7 horizontal rows, with 5 blocks in each row. Arrange blocks to get a nice balance of color and value. When satisfied with layout, join blocks in each row. Press.

2. Join rows.

Borders

1. See page 133 for tips on sewing a mitered border. Sew white border strips to quilt sides; miter corners.

2. Make templates of Border Scallop Pattern and Border Corner Pattern.

3. From muslin, cut 10 (4½"-wide) cross-grain strips. Sew 3 strips end-to-end for each side border and 2 strips each for top and bottom borders. Press seam allowances open.

4. Fold 1 longer muslin strip in half to find center. Position scallop template on fold, aligning straight edges of template with fabric edges. Trace curve onto muslin. Flip template to align straight edges with fabric and first tracing to trace next curve *(Diagram D)*. Continue working toward end of muslin strip, tracing

Quilt by Wanda Kertis of Belvidere, Illinois

pattern 8 times. At end, align and trace corner template. Return to center and repeat tracing for opposite end of strip. Mark second long muslin strip in same manner.

5. Mark shorter muslin strips in same manner, marking 6 scallop patterns on each side of center and ending with corner tracing.

6. Matching centers, pin marked strips to quilt to check fit. Adjust

corners as necessary. Remove muslin strips from quilt.

7. From remaining scrap strips, cut approximately 360 (4½"-long) pieces, ranging from 1" wide to 2" wide. Precise number needed will vary with random size of strings.

8. Start string piecing at center of each muslin strip. Lay down 1 string, aligning top and bottom edges with muslin. Place next string

Diagram D

on first, right sides facing, and stitch ¼" seam through all 3 layers. Press. Add next strip and continue string piecing up to corner. Angle pieces as desired to work around corner. Return to center and string-piece remainder of strip to opposite corner. String-piece 4 muslin strips in this manner. Do not cut scallops until quilting is complete.

9. Matching centers, sew each strip to quilt side. Miter corners.

Quilting and Finishing

1. Mark quilting design on quilt top as desired. On quilt shown, string piecing is outline-quilted. Quilting pattern for C triangles is at right. Wanda Kertis quilted undulating feathers in white center border. Look for a stencil of a similar design at your local quilt shop or in mail-order catalogs (see page 144), making sure stencil width will fit your border. Or create your own border quilting design.

2. Divide backing into 2 equal lengths. See page 135 for instructions on making a backing.

3. Layer backing, batting, and quilt top. Baste. Quilt as desired.

4. Carefully trim scalloped border, cutting through all layers.

5. Use narrow binding for scalloped edges. See page 139 for instructions on making continuous bias binding. From a 30" square of binding fabric, cut 12 yards of 2"-wide bias.

6. Fold and press binding as described on page 140.

7. Starting at center of any side, stitch binding to quilt top through all layers. Smooth bias around curves, being sure not to pull bias too tight.

8. Turn binding to wrong side and hand-stitch on backing. If necessary, clip seam allowance to smooth curves.

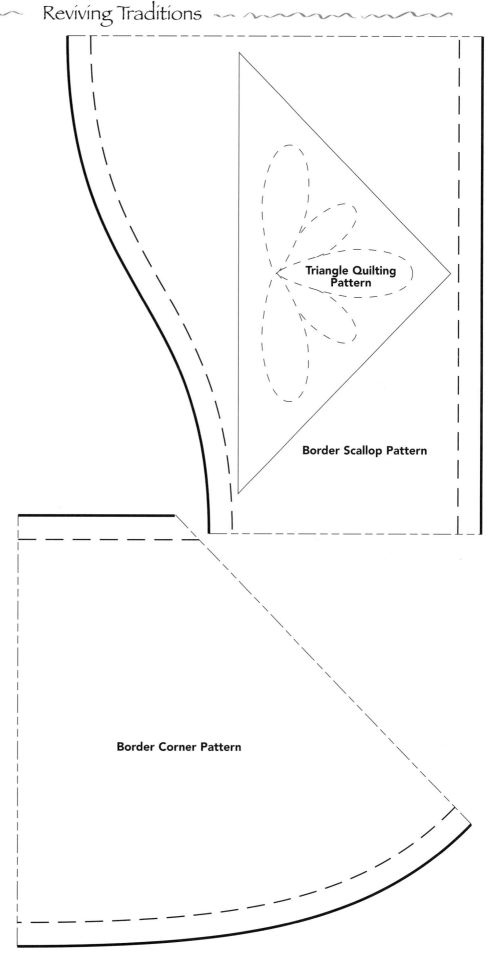

Triangle Quilting Pattern

Border Scallop Pattern

Border Corner Pattern

Spiral Feathered Star

These spinning wheels combine two challenges favored by lovers of exceptional piecework—curved seams and precise, narrow points. Enjoy working with scraps to reproduce this 1940s vintage quilt or choose your own color scheme to make an even more graphic statement.

Finished Size: 69" x 80½"
Blocks: 42 (11½" x 11½")

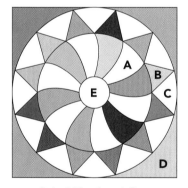

Spiral Feathered Star Block—Make 42.

Materials

5½ yards muslin
42 (¼-yard) print fabrics or scraps
¾ yard binding fabric
2⅛ yards 90"-wide backing fabric

Cutting

See page 126 for tips on making templates for piecing. Window templates are recommended to mark seam lines on wrong side of each piece. Make templates of patterns A–E on page 87.

From muslin, cut:
252 of Pattern A.
504 of Pattern C.
42 of Pattern E.

From scraps, cut:
252 of Pattern A.
504 of Pattern B.
168 of Pattern D.

Making Blocks

See page 88 for tips on stitching a curved seam. Refer to *Block Assembly Diagram* throughout.

1. Select 6 scrap A pieces for each block. Sew each piece to a muslin A piece *(Diagram A)*. Press seam allowances toward scraps.

2. Join A pairs to make inner circle.

3. Select 12 each of pieces B and C. Stitch B/C pairs *(Diagram B)*. Press seam allowances toward Cs.

4. Join B/C pairs to make outer circle.

5. Pin A circle to B/C circle, right sides facing. Clip seam allowances if necessary. Stitch circles together. Press.

6. Add 4 D pieces to outside edges of block, carefully following drawn seam line on wrong side of each piece. Press seam allowances toward Ds.

7. Piece or appliqué E over A seam allowances at block center.

8. Make 42 Spiral Feathered Star blocks.

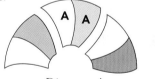

Diagram A

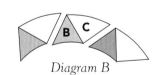

Diagram B

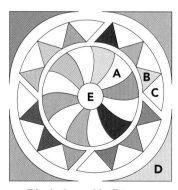

Block Assembly Diagram

I've been a hard worker all my life . . . but most all my work has been the kind that perishes with the using. But when one of my grandchildren sees one of these quilts, they'll think about Aunt Jane, and wherever I am then, I'll know I ain't forgotten.

—*Aunt Jane of Kentucky* by Eliza Calvert Hall

Quilt Assembly

Referring to photo, join blocks in 7 horizontal rows with 6 blocks in each row. Join rows.

Quilting and Finishing

1. Mark desired quilting design on top. Quilt shown is outline-quilted.

2. Layer backing, batting, and quilt top. Baste. Quilt as desired.

3. Make 8½ yards of binding. See page 139 for instructions on making and applying binding.

Antique quilt owned by Becky Herdle of Rochester, New York

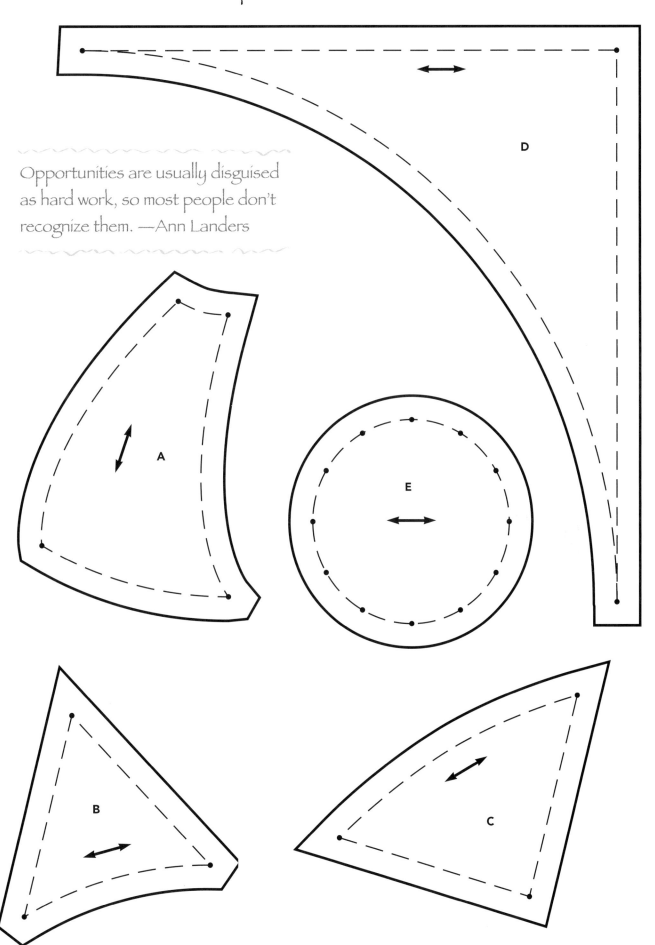

Opportunities are usually disguised
as hard work, so most people don't
recognize them. —Ann Landers

Piecing a Curved Seam

Piecing curves doesn't have to be difficult. It just requires a little extra care to ensure a smooth seam. Try both methods described here to see which technique you like best.

Machine Piecing

1. Make small clips in curved edge of one D piece. Be careful not to cut into seam line. Clips let seam allowance spread so curved edges will match for piecing.
2. Match D to pieced circle, right sides facing. Pin curved edges together (*Diagram A*). Let piece gather as necessary, but make it as smooth as possible at curved edge.
3. With D piece on top, machine-stitch seam. Start at one end and carefully sew around curve, smoothing creases away from seam as you stitch. Remove each pin

before you stitch over it.
4. Press seam allowance toward D (*Diagram B*). If necessary, a hot steam iron can work out tiny puckers in seam.

Hand Piecing

1. Referring to page 126, make a window template for Pattern D. Cut D pieces, marking seam line on wrong side of each piece.
2. Clip and pin pieces as described for machine piecing.
3. Make a knot in end of sewing thread. Bring up needle to start stitching at one end of seam line.
4. Making a small running stitch, carefully sew along marked seam line. Remove pins as you go.
5. At end of seam, knot off thread.
6. Press seam allowance toward D (*Diagram B*).

Diagram A

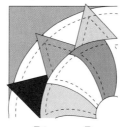

Diagram B

I've had a heap of comfort all my life making quilts, and now in my old age, I wouldn't take a fortune for them. —*Aunt Jane of Kentucky* by Eliza Calvert Hall

No woman should be shamefaced in attempting to give back to the world, through her work, a portion of its lost heart.—Louise Bogan, poet, 1898–1970

If art doesn't make us better, then what on earth is it for? —Alice Walker

Bias Appliqué

Make curvy appliquéd vines and flower stems from bias strips. Use bias pressing bars of metal or heat-resistant plastic to prepare lengths of bias for appliqué. Available in various widths, bias bars are sold at quilt shops and through mail-order catalogs (see page 144).

1. Start with a fabric square. Quilt instructions give size of square and width of strips to be cut. Cut square in half diagonally to get two large triangles.

2. See page 139 for instructions on making continuous bias. For stems, it's usually easier to cut bias strips, measuring from cut edge of each triangle *(Photo A)*.

3. Fold strip in half lengthwise, wrong sides facing and long edges together. Stitch ¼" from edges, making a narrow tube.

4. Slide each tube onto pressing bar, centering seam on flat side of bar *(Photo B)*.

5. Press seam allowance to one side or open, as you prefer *(Photo C)*. Handle metal bars carefully—they get hot! Remove bar when pressing is complete. Trim seam allowance if necessary.

6. With seam against background fabric, baste or pin bias strip in place *(Photo D)*. A steam iron will help shape curves. Appliqué strip onto background fabric, sewing inside curves first and then outside curves so that bias lies flat.

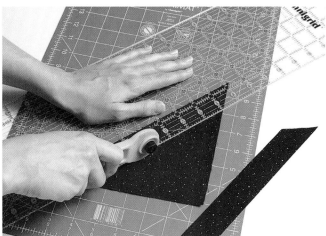

A

B

C

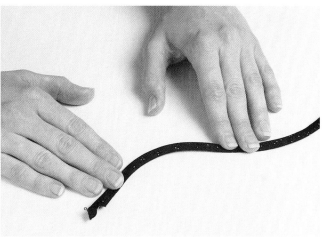

D

Princess Feathers

Time-honored traditions are evident here: a four-block set, a fancy border, and the red, white, and green color scheme that is sparked with a colonial-era cheddar color. It's all set off with Gerry Sweem's beautiful hand quilting, which makes it a classic for the ages.

Finished Size: 80" x 80"
Blocks: 4 (31" x 31")

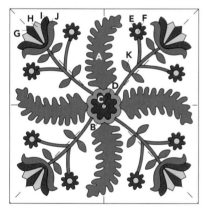

Princess Feathers Block 1—Make 2.

Princess Feathers Block 2—Make 2.

Materials

6 yards white
2¼ yards red (includes binding)
1¾ yards green print A
1½ yards green print B
⅝ yard cheddar
½ yard green print C
⅜ yard pink print
2½ yards 90"-wide backing fabric
½"-wide bias pressing bar

Cutting

See page 126 for tips on cutting pieces for hand appliqué. Make templates of patterns A–K on pages 92–95. Cut pieces in order listed to make best use of yardage.

From white, cut:
4 (32") squares.
4 (9¼" x 86") lengthwise strips for borders.

From red, cut:
30" square for binding.
8 of Pattern C.
48 of Pattern E.
24 of Pattern G.
24 of Pattern I.

From green print A, cut:
8 of Pattern A.
8 of Pattern A reversed.

From green print B, cut:
36" square for stems.
24 of Pattern J.

From cheddar, cut:
48 of Pattern F.
24 of Pattern H.
8 of Pattern D.

From green print C, cut:
64 of Pattern K.
64 of Pattern K reversed.

From pink, cut:
8 of Pattern B.

Making Blocks

Blocks 1 and 2 are the same except for direction of spinning A feathers.

1. See tip box on Bias Appliqué to prepare stems (page 89). Cut 36" square of green print B in half diagonally; then cut 1½"-wide diagonal strips. Fold, stitch, and press as instructed, finishing with ½"-wide bias strips.

2. From prepared bias strips, cut 16 (12") lengths and 32 (5¼") lengths for blocks. Set remainder aside for border. (It is not necessary to turn under stem ends, as these are covered by other pieces.)

3. See page 131 for tips on preparing cut pieces for hand appliqué. Do not turn under edges that will be covered by other pieces, such as narrow ends of leaves or straight ends of feathers. Clip seam allowances as necessary to achieve nice points and smooth curves.

4. For each block, center and appliqué C flower onto B flower; then appliqué D center. If desired, trim B fabric under C appliqué to reduce fabric layers for quilting, leaving ¼" seam allowance.

5. Prepare 32 E/F flowers (8 for each block), appliquéing F centers onto each E piece. $\longrightarrow$

6. Fold each white square in half vertically, horizontally, and diagonally, creasing or lightly pressing folds to make placement guides for appliqué *(Diagram A)*.

7. Referring to block diagram, pin or baste appliqué pieces onto each square. Center B flower; then align A feathers and long stems with placement guides, tucking ends under B. *(Note: A reversed feathers are used in 2 blocks; be sure not to get feather types mixed up in same block.)* Position G, H, I, and J pieces for tulips at stem ends, aligning G diamond with diagonal placement line. Tuck ends of short stems under long stem at its midpoint; then pin E/F flowers at stem ends. Tuck blunt ends of 2 K leaves under each long stem, about ¾" below short stems.

8. When satisfied with placement of pieces on each block, stitch leaves and short stems in place. Then sew long stems and A feathers. Finally, appliqué tulip pieces and B flowers.

9. Make 2 of Block 1 and 2 of Block 2 as shown. Press each appliquéd block.

10. Using D as center, trim each block to 31½" square.

Quilt Assembly

1. Referring to photo, join blocks in 2 rows of 2 blocks each; then join rows to make a 62½" square. Press seam allowances open or to 1 side as desired.

2. Referring to page 133, sew borders to joined blocks; miter corners.

3. From prepared bias strips, cut 8 each of 18½", 12½", and 6" lengths.

4. Prepare 64 K leaves, 4 B/C/D flowers, 8 G/H/I/J tulips, and 16 E/F flowers.

5. Referring to photo, pin flowers, stems, and leaves on border. Start with B corner flowers, centering Ds on mitered seams about 5½" from inside corner of quilt. Pin each tulip directly opposite a block tulip, placing tip of I pieces about 2" apart (1" on either side of border seam). Use pinned flowers to anchor remaining pieces, tucking 12½" stems under B flowers and 18½" stems under each tulip. Pin a 6" stem in place at midpoint of longer stem. Pin remaining pieces in place as shown.

6. When satisfied with placement of pieces, appliqué in place. Start with leaves; then stitch stems. Appliqué flowers last.

Quilting and Finishing

1. Mark quilting design on quilt top as desired. On quilt shown, Gerry Sweem hand-quilted double lines of outline quilting around each appliqué piece and triple diagonal lines on each block that angle into center of quilt (middle lines are 1" apart). Border seam is enhanced with lovely curving quilted feathers. At borders and quilt centers where tulips come together, Gerry quilted a curving flower. Flower Quilting Pattern is on page 95. See page 134 for tips on making your own quilting stencil.

2. Layer backing, batting, and quilt top. Baste. Quilt as desired.

3. Make 9¼ yards of binding. See page 139 for instructions on making and applying binding.

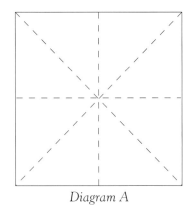

Diagram A

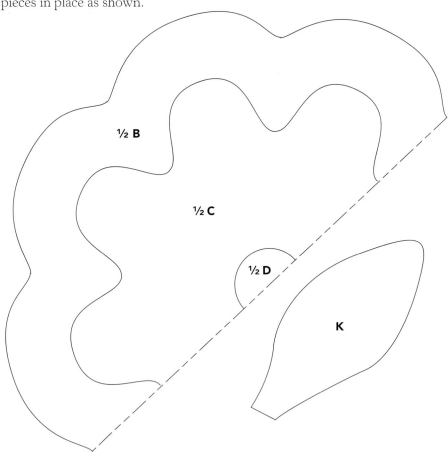

½ B

½ C

½ D

K

Quilt by Gerry Sweem of Reseda, California

Why is this design called Princess Feathers? We can't be quite sure, but one theory has it that the design is derived from the insignia of Britain's Prince of Wales—a coronet topped with three curving plumes. What might once have been known as the Prince's feathers has, over time, evolved into the design we know as Princess Feathers.

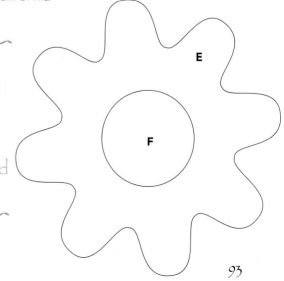

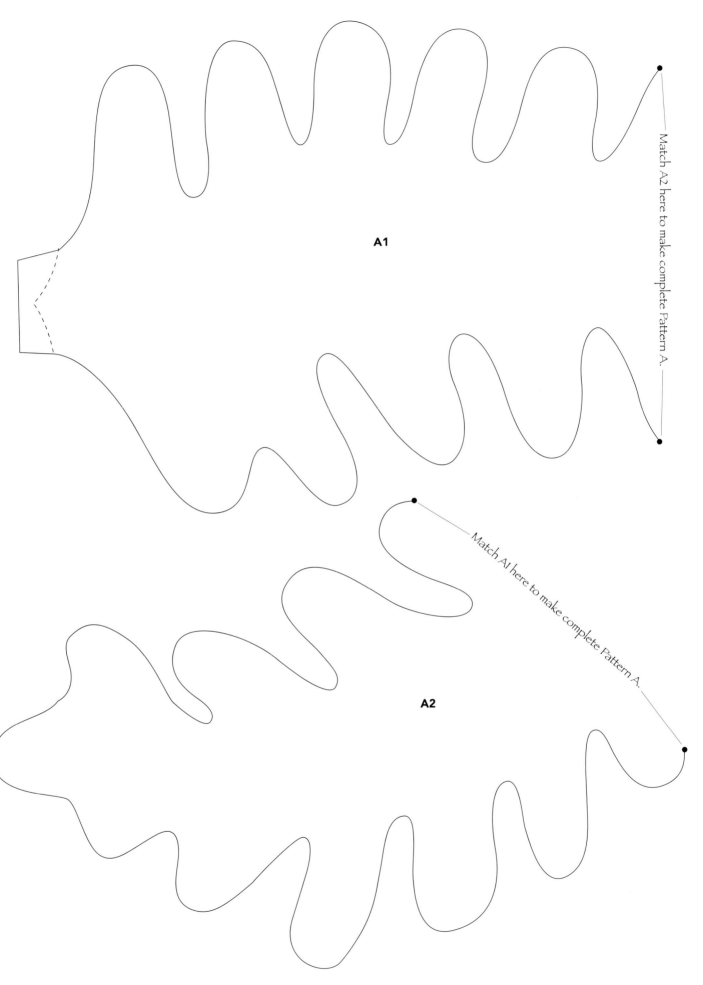

A1

Match A2 here to make complete Pattern A.

A2

Match A1 here to make complete Pattern A.

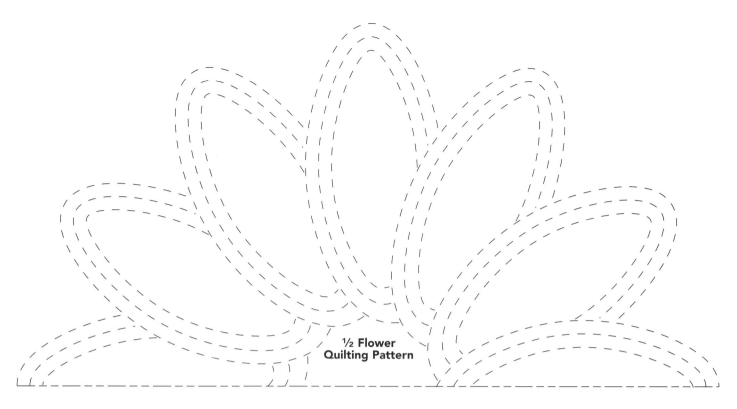

½ **Flower**
Quilting Pattern

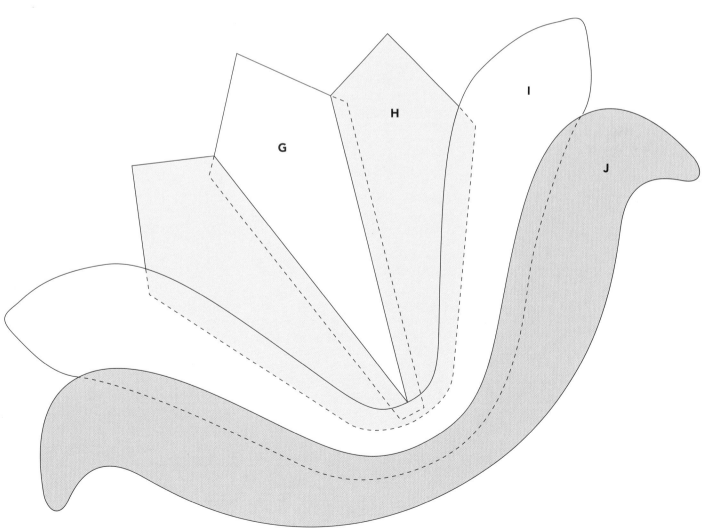

G

H

I

J

Breaking Away

Shed your inhibitions, throw away the rule
book, and discover how exciting fabric can be.
There are wonderful prints and patterns in the
stores these days, and many are *not* the kind
of material *your* grandmother used. Be daring
with these bold, exciting new fabrics—they'll
help you create a one-of-a-kind quilt.

Forgive, O Lord, my little jokes on thee,
And I'll forgive thy big one on me.
—Robert Frost

Summer Sunshine,
page 108

Hummingbird's Delight

For Terry Benzo, there's no such thing as too many fabrics. She used lots of floral prints and a traditional, easy-to-sew Courthouse Steps block to make a dramatic quilt that proves the importance of value.

Finished Size: 79" x 79"
Blocks: 113 (7" x 7")

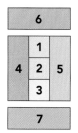

Block 1—Make 81.

Block 2—Make 32.

Materials

(see Tips on Value below)
23 (1½"-wide) strips light fabrics
34 (1½"-wide) strips light/medium fabrics
9 (1½"-wide) strips medium fabrics
63 (1½"-wide) strips medium/dark fabrics
20 (1½"-wide) strips dark fabrics
2 (⅜-yard) dark fabrics or scraps for setting triangles
⅜ yard accent border fabric*
1 yard binding fabric
5 yards backing fabric
* *Note:* The color of the accent border becomes the dominant color of the quilt. Terry's quilt seems to have a predominance of red, but there's really no more red than any other color—it's the border that emphasizes the quilt's red fabrics. Choose an accent fabric accordingly.

Tips on Value

This quilt uses up lots of scraps. Cut cross-grain strips of miscellaneous print fabrics and sort them by value.

Value refers to a fabric's relative lightness or darkness. While some fabrics are obviously dark and some are obviously light, many fall somewhere in between. And a medium can read as light or dark, depending on the value of its neighbors.

Sort strips into value groups of light, light/medium, medium, medium/dark, and dark. Cast some medium fabrics in the role of a dark or light—surrounded by darks, the fabric will appear to be light; the same fabric, surrounded by lights, appears to be dark.

Blocks 1 and 2

Block 1 is mostly light, while Block 2 is mostly dark. Both blocks are sewn in the same manner. Refer to block diagrams throughout.
1. Block 1 uses light fabrics in positions 1–5, light/medium fabrics in positions 6–9, and medium/dark fabrics in positions 10–13. Select 13 fabric strips for first block.
2. Cut a 1½" square from each of 3 light fabrics. Join 3 squares to form block center (Diagram A).
3. Cut a 3½"-long piece each from remaining 2 light fabrics. Sew these to sides of center unit (4 and 5 in diagram). Press seam allowances away from center.
4. From 2 light/medium fabrics, cut 3½"-long pieces for 6 and 7. Sew these to top and bottom of center unit (Diagram B). Press seam allowances away from center. ⟶

Diagram A   *Diagram B*

5. Cut 5½"-long pieces for 8 and 9 from 2 more light/medium fabrics. Sew these to sides of center unit (*Diagram C*).

6. From medium/dark fabrics, cut 5½"-long pieces for 10 and 11; then cut 7½"-long pieces for 12 and 13. Sew pieces in place as shown, pressing each seam allowance away from center.

7. Make 81 of Block 1 in this manner, adding strips in numerical order as shown.

8. For Block 2, use medium fabrics for 1–5, medium/dark fabrics for 6–9, and dark fabrics for 10–13. Make 32 of Block 2.

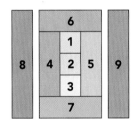

Diagram C

Quilt Assembly Diagram

Quilt Assembly

Blocks 1 and 2 are joined in diagonal rows with setting triangles at row ends. Accent border is appliquéd over assembled quilt.

1. From dark fabrics, cut 7 (11¼") squares. Cut each square in quarters diagonally to get 28 setting triangles. From remaining dark fabric, cut 2 (6") squares. Cut these in half diagonally to get 4 corner triangles.

2. Lay out blocks in diagonal rows, indicated by dark lines (*Quilt Assembly Diagram*). Except for middle row, each row has 1 setting triangle and 1 of Block 2 at each end. Middle row has 2 of Block 2 and corner triangles at each end as shown. Distribute blocks as desired to get a nice balance of color and values.

3. When satisfied with arrangement of blocks, join blocks in each row.

4. Join rows as shown.

5. Cut 6 (1½"-wide) cross-grain strips for accent border. Join strips end-to-end to make a strip approximately 6⅝ yards long.

6. Fold border strip in half lengthwise, wrong sides facing. Use ¼" seam allowance to join raw edges.

7. Press seam allowances open, centering seam on 1 side.

8. Starting at any corner, pin border on top of dark blocks as shown (*Quilt Assembly Diagram*), mitering corners. When satisfied with placement, appliqué border in place.

Quilting and Finishing

1. Mark quilting design on quilt top as desired. On quilt shown, Terry Benzo outline-quilted accent border and machine-quilted a loose, meandering stipple-like design on quilt surface.

2. Divide backing fabric into 2 equal lengths. See page 135 for instructions on making a backing.

3. Layer backing, batting, and quilt top. Baste. Quilt as desired.

4. Make 9 yards of binding. See page 139 for instructions on making and applying binding.

5. Terry cut hummingbird figures from a novelty fabric and appliquéd the birds here and there on the surface of her quilt (see photo). If desired, find a novelty fabric you like (horses, chickens, cats, children), and appliqué figures on quilt top as desired.

Quilt by Terry Benzo of Pittsburgh, Pennsylvania

Star Ripples

Using only straight seams and the magic of color value, this design creates the illusion of curves. The formula combines a consistent accent fabric with scraps in two color families, ranging from very light to very dark.

Finished Size: 43" x 43"
Blocks: 9 (10" x 10")

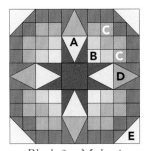

Block 1—Make 5.

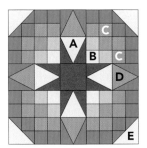

Block 2—Make 4.

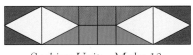

Sashing Unit—Make 12.

Materials

⅛-yard pieces *each* or scraps of 23 greens and 23 blues, ranging from very light to very dark
½ yard bright pink
⅜ yard light pink
½ yard inner border fabric (includes binding)
½ yard outer border fabric
1¼ yards backing fabric

Cutting

Lay out blue and green fabrics from lightest to darkest. Some distinctions will be easy, but sometimes it's difficult to determine if one fabric is really darker than the next. Line up the fabrics in a row, stand back, and squint a little—you'll be able to see better if one is out of order. Assign each fabric a number, starting with the lightest as #1. (For placement of each numbered fabric, see individual unit diagrams.)

Rotary cutting instructions for scrap fabrics are listed from lightest to darkest, or from 1 to 23. Quantities for green blocks are given, followed by blue block requirements in brackets. You can cut all pieces before you begin, or cut pieces for each unit as you sew. Refer to diagrams throughout these instructions to identify units.

Cut all strips cross-grain.

From Green 1 [Blue 1], cut:
1 (2¾"-wide) strip. From this, cut 20 [16] triangles for Unit 1A [2A]. Align 60° line on ruler with bottom edge of strip to cut equilateral triangles (*Diagrams A and B*).

From each of next 8 greens [blues], cut:
20 [16] 1½" squares for units 1B [2B] and 1C [2C].

From Green 10 [Blue 10], cut:
1 (2¾"-wide) strip. From this, cut 20 [16] triangles for Unit 1D [2D] as before.

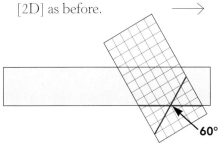

Diagram A

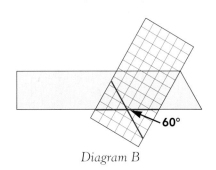

Diagram B

If you're going to make a mistake, make a doozy. And don't be afraid to hit the ball. —Billie Jean King

From greens 11 and 12 [blues 11 and 12], cut:

1 (3⅜"-wide) strip. From each strip, cut 10 [8] 1⅝" x 3⅜" rectangles. Cut 1 set of rectangles in half diagonally to get 20 [16] triangles for Unit 1D [2D] (Diagram C). Cut remaining rectangles in other direction to get 10 [8] reversed triangles for Unit 1D [2D]. Trim ⅞" from tip of each triangle as shown.

From each of next 5 greens [blues], cut:

20 [16] 1½" squares for units 1C [2C] and 1E [2E].

From greens [blues] 18 and 19, cut:

10 [8] 1⅞" squares. Cut each square in half to get small triangles for Unit 1E [2E].

From greens [blues] 20 and 21, cut:

12 (1½") squares for Unit 3C.

From greens [blues] 22 and 23, cut:

1 (3⅜"-wide) strip. From each strip, cut 12 (1⅝" x 3⅜") rectangles. Cut 6 of each set of rectangles in half diagonally to get 24 triangles (12 of each color) for Unit 3B (Diagram C). Cut remaining rectangles in other direction to get 24 reversed triangles for Unit 3D. Trim ⅞" from tip of each triangle.

From bright pink, cut:

13 (2½") squares for blocks and sashing.

8 (1½" x 2½") pieces for border sashing.

4 (1½") squares for corners.

6 (1⅝"-wide) strips. From these, cut 72 (1⅝" x 3⅜") rectangles. Cut 36 rectangles in half diagonally in 1 direction; then cut remaining 36 rectangles in opposite direction (Diagram C) to cut 144 triangles for units 1A, 2A, 3A, 4A, and 4D.

From light pink, cut:

2 (2⅞"-wide) strips. From these, cut 18 (2⅞") squares. Cut each square in half to get 72 triangles for units 1E and 2E.

2 (2¾"-wide) strips. From these, cut 48 equilateral triangles as before for units 3A, 3B, and 3D.

1 (3⅜"-wide) strip. From this, cut 24 (1⅝" x 3⅜") rectangles. Cut 12 rectangles in half in 1 direction; then cut remaining rectangles in opposite direction (Diagram C) to get 48 triangles for border sashing units.

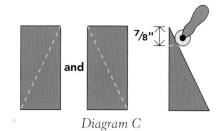

Diagram C

Unit 1A— Make 20.

Unit 1B— Make 20.

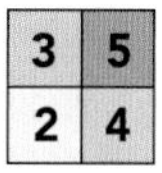

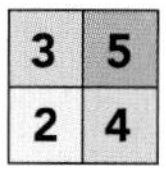

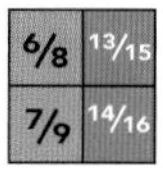

Unit 1C—Make 40 (20 each of 2 sets).

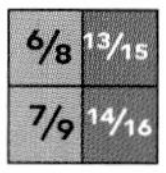

Unit 1D— Make 20.

Unit 1E— Make 20.

Unit 2A— Make 16.

Unit 2B— Make 16.

Unit 2C—Make 32 (16 each of 2 sets).

Unit 2D— Make 16.

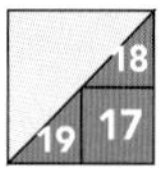

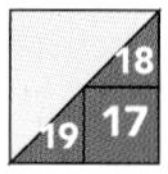

Unit 2E— Make 16.

Blocks 1 and 2

Make 1 block to verify fabric placement; then make additional blocks to match. Refer to unit diagrams throughout.

1. Use Green 1 triangles and bright pink triangles to make 4 of Unit 1A as shown. Press seam allowances toward bright pink.

2. For Unit 1B, join squares of greens 2, 3, 4, and 5 to make a four-patch as shown. Make 4 of Unit 1B.

3. For Unit 1C, join squares of greens 6, 7, 13, and 14 to make a four-patch as shown. Make 4 four-patches of this fabric combination. Make 4 more four-patches using squares of greens 8, 9, 15, and 16.

4. For Unit 1D, sew triangles of fabrics 11 and 12 to Green 10 triangles. Press seam allowances toward outer triangles. Make 4 of Unit 1D.

5. For Unit 1E, sew triangles of greens 18 and 19 to Green 17 square. Press seam allowances toward triangles. Add light pink triangle as shown. Make 4 of Unit 1E.

6. Lay out units in 5 horizontal rows as shown (Block 1 Assembly Diagram). Position different C units so that same sets are not in same row or at adjacent corners (see photo). Include bright pink 2½" square in third row for star center.

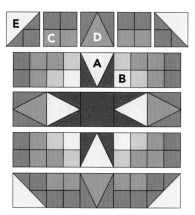

Block 1 Assembly Diagram

7. When satisfied with position of each unit, join units in each row. In rows 1, 3, and 5, press joining seam allowances toward center of row. In rows 2 and 4, press seam allowances away from center.

8. Join rows to complete Block 1.
9. In this manner, make 5 of Block 1 and 4 of Block 2. ⟶

Quilt by Nancy Graves of Manhattan, Kansas

Sashing

1. Use light pink and bright pink triangles to make 24 of Unit 3A as shown (*Sashing Assembly Diagram*). Press seam allowances toward outer triangles.

2. Sew green and blue 22 and 23 triangles to light pink triangle in same manner to make 12 each of units 3B and 3D. Be sure to position fabrics correctly for each unit.

3. For unit 3C, use squares of fabrics 20 and 21 to make a four-patch. Make 4 of Unit 3C.

4. Join units 3A, 3B, 3C, 3D, and 3A in a row as shown to make 1 sashing unit. Make 12 sashing units.

5. Assemble Border Sashing units 1 and 2 in same manner as shown. Make 8 of Border Sashing Unit 1 and 4 of Border Sashing Unit 2.

6. You should have now used all cut pieces except 4 large squares, 4 small corner squares, and 8 rectangles, all in bright pink.

Sashing Assembly Diagram

Border Sashing Unit 1—Make 8.

Border Sashing Unit 2—Make 4.

Quilt Assembly

1. Lay out blocks in 3 horizontal rows with 3 blocks in each row (*Row Assembly Diagram*). Place sashing units between blocks, turning sashing to align green and blue fabrics with adjacent blocks. Place border sashing units at ends of each row as shown.

2. Lay out sashing rows between block rows, using bright pink squares between sashing units and rectangles at row ends.

3. Lay out border sashing rows at top and bottom as shown.

4. When satisfied with placement of all units, join blocks and sashing units in each row. Then join rows.

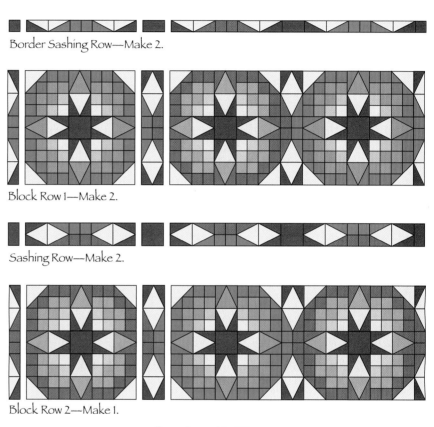

Border Sashing Row—Make 2.

Block Row 1—Make 2.

Sashing Row—Make 2.

Block Row 2—Make 1.

Row Assembly Diagram

I make time for quilting by eating out and only cleaning house every other week. When I die, the house will be dirty in a few days anyway, so I might as well spend my time quilting.—Nancy Graves, Manhattan, Kansas

Borders

1. From inner border fabric, cut 4 (1" x 38") strips.

2. Referring to page 132, measure quilt from top to bottom through middle of quilt. Trim 2 border strips to match length. Sew these to quilt sides. Press seam allowances toward borders.

3. Measure quilt from side to side through middle of quilt. Trim remaining borders to match quilt width. Sew trimmed borders to top and bottom edges. Press seam allowances toward borders.

4. Cut 4 (3½"-wide) strips of outer border fabric. Repeat steps 2 and 3 to add outer border.

Quilting and Finishing

1. Mark quilting design on quilt top as desired. On quilt shown, Nancy Graves quilted concentric circles around stars in each block and a meandering ripple in outer borders.

2. Layer backing, batting, and quilt top. Baste. Quilt as desired.

3. Use remaining inner border fabric to make 5 yards of straight-grain binding. See page 139 for instructions on making and applying binding.

Why I Quilt
by Beverly Leasure, Dunedin, Florida

It was humiliating. There I was, newly married and spending our first Christmas with my husband's family. I wanted to make a good impression. So imagine my horror as, with all my in-laws watching, I opened a large package from my mother and pulled out the ugliest quilt you ever saw.

My embarrasment deepened as everyone insisted that I open it up to its full size. The sashing and border fabric was a garish bright turquoise. The patchwork was every color under the sun. The backing was a fuchsia that even overpowered the turquoise.

Mother didn't know the first thing about making a quilt. And it showed. It was awful. But her quilt was made with love, so it became part of our family life.

In time, "Grandma's Quilt" put in yeoman's service. It travelled on family car trips and to many a picnic. It made a great fort when draped over some chairs. It was machine washed more times than I care to count. And that ugly quilt had a magic that defies explanation.

When a child was sick, Grandma's quilt was part of the cure. When it was wrapped around you, you automatically felt better. It was also a great comfort when the world wasn't a nice place.

The quilt is in shreds now—whenever we use it, pieces fall on the floor. Someday there will be nothing of it left. For now, however, even though my children are grown, it still has magic powers. I can't remember if I ever told my mother how great was her gift to us.

I started quilting in 1985, largely because of that precious, hideous quilt. I've learned all the right techniques, and now I can piece and quilt with the best. My points come together nicely. I know about color theory and value. But I don't know if the quilts I make will ever have the magical powers of Grandma's quilt.

Summer Sunshine

A splashy fabric and sparkling metallic threads bring the sizzle of summer to this quick-pieced wall hanging. Use a big, bright print like this to liberate a traditional design and establish a theme for the overall work.

Finished Size: 59" x 59"
Blocks: 16 (9" x 9") • 16 (6" x 9")

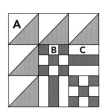

Block 1—Make 12.

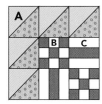

Block 2—Make 4.

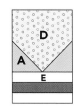

Block 3—Make 16.

Materials

⅝ yard Green 1
1¾ yards Green 2 (includes outer border)
1¼ yards muslin
1 yard blue
1 yard theme print
½ yard yellow
½ yard binding fabric
3¼ yards backing fabric

Cutting

Instructions are for strip cutting and quick piecing. Cut all strips cross-grain unless lengthwise grain is specified.

From Green 1, cut:
6 (6" x 21½") strips for Block 1 triangle-squares.

From Green 2, cut:
4 (4¼" x 63") lengthwise strips for outer border.
2 (6" x 21½") strips for Block 2 triangle-squares.

From muslin, cut:
15 (1½"-wide) strips for strip sets 1 and 2.
6 (6" x 21½") strips for Block 1 triangle-squares.

From blue, cut:
5 (2"-wide) strips for inner border.
11 (1½"-wide) strips for strip sets 1 and 2.

From theme print, cut:
20 (6½") D squares.

From yellow, cut:
2 (6" x 21½") strips for Block 2 triangle-squares.
32 (3½") A squares for Block 3.

Block 1

See General Instructions, pages 129 and 130, for step-by-step instructions for strip piecing and quick-pieced triangle-squares.

1. On wrong side of each 6" x 21½" muslin piece, draw a 1-square by 5-square grid of 3⅞" squares *(Diagram A)*. Mark diagonal lines through squares as shown.

2. Match each marked piece with a strip of Green 1 fabric, right sides facing. Stitch on both sides of diagonal lines, pivoting at corners as shown. Press stitching. Cut on all drawn lines to get 10 triangle-squares from each grid (5 for each of 12 blocks). Press seam allowances toward green.

3. Join muslin and blue strips to make 6 of Strip Set 1 and 2 of Strip Set 2 *(Strip Set Diagrams)*. For third Strip Set 2, cut remaining blue and muslin strips in half to make half a strip set. Press seam allowances toward blue.

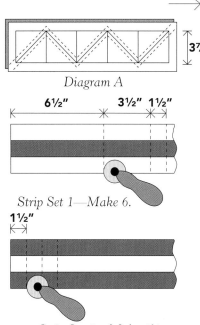

Diagram A

Strip Set 1—Make 6.

Strip Set 2—Make 2½.

4. From Strip Set 1, cut 16 (6½"-wide) E segments. Set Es aside for Block 3. Then cut 32 (3½"-wide) C segments and 32 (1½"-wide) segments for blocks 1 and 2.

5. From Strip Set 2, cut 64 (1½"-wide) segments.

6. Join 2 Set 2 segments and 1 (1½"-wide) Set 1 segment to make a nine-patch (B) as shown *(Diagram B)*. Make 32 nine-patch units. Set aside 8 units for Block 2.

7. For each Block 1, select 5 A triangle-squares, 2 B nine-patch units, and 2 (3½"-wide) Strip Set 1 segments (C). Join units in 3 horizontal rows as shown *(Block 1 Assembly Diagram)*. Join rows to complete block.

8. Make 12 of Block 1.

Block 2

1. Use 6" x 21½" strips of Green 2 and yellow fabrics to make triangle-squares as before. Stitch 2 grids to get 20 A triangle-squares, 5 for each of 4 blocks.

2. For each block, select 5 A triangle-squares, 2 B nine-patch units, and 2 (3½"-wide) Strip Set 1 segments (C). Join units in 3 rows as before. Join rows to complete block.

3. Make 4 of Block 2.

Block 3

See General Instructions, page 128, for illustrated step-by-step instructions for sewing diagonal corners.

1. Use diagonal-corner technique to sew 2 yellow A squares to 16 D squares of theme fabric as shown *(Diagram C)*.

2. Join theme fabric unit to 6½"-wide segment of Strip Set 1 (E) to complete block as shown.

3. Make 16 of Block 3.

Quilt Assembly

1. For Row 1, lay out 4 of Block 1 and 2 of Block 3 as shown *(Quilt Assembly Diagram)*. Join blocks in a row as shown. Press seam allowances toward Block 3. Make 2 of Row 1.

2. For Row 2, select 4 of Block 3 and 2 extra theme fabric squares. Join units in a row as shown. Press seam allowances toward Block 3. Make 2 of Row 2.

3. For Row 3, select 2 each of blocks 1, 2, and 3. Join blocks in a row as shown. Press seam allowances toward Block 3. Make 2 of Row 3.

4. Join 1 each of rows 1, 2, and 3 for top half of quilt. Repeat to make bottom half. Turn bottom half upside down to join it to top half (see photo).

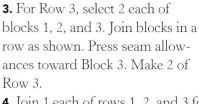

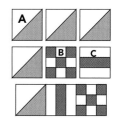

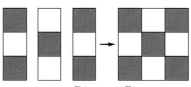

Diagram B

Block 1 Assembly Diagram

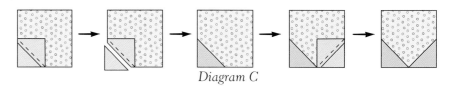

Diagram C

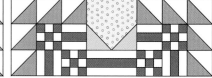

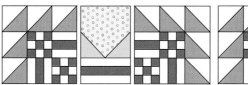

Row 1—Make 2.

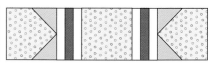

Row 2—Make 2.

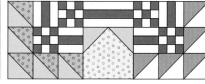

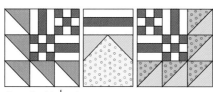

Row 3—Make 2.

Quilt Assembly Diagram

In the last two decades, I've lost 789 pounds. I should be hanging from a charm bracelet. —Erma Bombeck

Borders

1. From 1 blue border strip, cut 4 (10"-long) segments. Sew 1 segment onto 1 end of each remaining blue border strip.

2. Referring to page 132, measure quilt from top to bottom through middle of quilt. Trim 2 blue strips to match length. Sew trimmed borders to quilt sides. Press seam allowances toward borders.

3. Measure quilt from side to side through middle of quilt. Trim remaining blue borders to match quilt width. Sew trimmed borders to top and bottom edges. Press seam allowances toward borders.

4. Repeat steps 2 and 3 to add outer border strips.

Quilting and Finishing

1. Mark quilting design on quilt top as desired. On quilt shown, Lila Scott used metallic thread to machine-quilt around motifs in her theme fabric. She added closely-worked stipple quilting in yellow triangles and a loose, meandering stipple in remaining areas.

2. Divide backing fabric into 2 equal lengths. See page 135 for instructions on making a backing.

3. Layer backing, batting, and quilt top. Baste. Quilt as desired.

4. Make 6¾ yards of straight-grain binding. See page 139 for instructions on making and applying binding.

5. See page 141 for tips on making a hanging sleeve.

Quilt by Lila Taylor Scott of Marietta, Georgia

Moon & Star Whimsy
Heavenly bodies flicker to life in this interesting quilt. Full moons, half-moons, and over-sized stars are framed by a wide snaking bias border.

Finished Size: 78" x 92½"
Blocks: 20 (14½" x 14½")

Moon & Stars Block—Make 20.

Materials
10 (⅜-yard) pieces or scraps for
   appliqué
5¼ yards cream print*
1 yard brown for bias border
1 yard binding fabric
5½ yards backing fabric
*Note: If prewashed fabric is not a
full 45" wide, you may need an
additional 1½ yards to cut blocks.

Cutting
See page 126 for tips on cutting
pieces for appliqué. Use template
plastic to trace each quadrant of
pattern on pages 116 and 117 to
make a complete pattern.
From cream print, cut:
4 (10½" x 80") lengthwise strips for
   borders.
20 (15") squares for blocks.
**From bias border and binding
fabrics, cut:**
1 (30") square of each. Add leftover
   fabric to scraps for appliqué.
From scraps, cut:
20 full moons.
36 stars.
22 half-moons.

Appliqué Blocks
See page 131 for tips on preparing
moons and stars for appliqué.
1. Center a full moon on each
cream square. Referring to photo,
vary position of moons. Appliqué.
2. Position a star in open circle of
each full moon. Appliqué.

Quilt Assembly
1. Referring to photo, lay out blocks
in 5 horizontal rows with 4 blocks in
each row, turning blocks as desired
to alter positions of moons and stars.
2. When satisfied with placement,
join blocks in each row.
3. Join rows.

Borders
1. Referring to page 132, measure
quilt from top to bottom through
middle of quilt. Trim 2 border
strips to match length. Sew
trimmed strips to quilt sides. Press
seam allowances toward borders.
2. Measure quilt from side to side
through middle of quilt. Trim
remaining borders to match quilt
width. Sew trimmed borders to top
and bottom edges. Press seam
allowances toward borders.
3. Fold quilt in half to find center.
Use a pin to mark center on outer
edge of each border.
4. See page 139 for instructions on
making continuous bias. Using
brown square, make 7½ yards of
2½"-wide bias.
5. Fold bias strip in half lengthwise,
wrong sides facing. Stitch a ¼"
seam through both layers. Press
seam allowance open, centering
seam on 1 side of strip.
6. Fold prepared bias strip in 8
equal lengths; mark each eighth
with a pin.   ⟶

Marriage is a great institution, but I'm not ready for an institution yet. —Mae West

7. Position bias on outer border, with seam allowance against quilt top. Start at a corner approximately 2" from edge of fabric. Match next pin to border center, about 2" from edge. Match subsequent pins on bias strip with corners and border centers. Referring to photo, curve bias into place on each border, pinning it in place as you go.

8. When satisfied with placement, appliqué bias in place. Trim excess bias where ends meet and overlap.

9. Scatter half-moons and stars on borders. Place 1 piece over bias ends to cover overlap. Appliqué.

Quilting and Finishing

1. Mark quilting design on quilt top as desired. Quilt shown has echo quilting inside each shape (concentric circles in full moon are ½" apart) and 1"-wide cross-hatching is quilted in background. Outline-quilt bias border.

2. Divide backing into 2 equal lengths. See page 135 for instructions on making a backing.

3. Layer backing, batting, and quilt top. Baste. Quilt as desired.

4. Make 9⅝ yards of binding. See page 139 for instructions on making and applying binding.

Quilt by Marion Roach Watchinski of Overland Park, Kansas

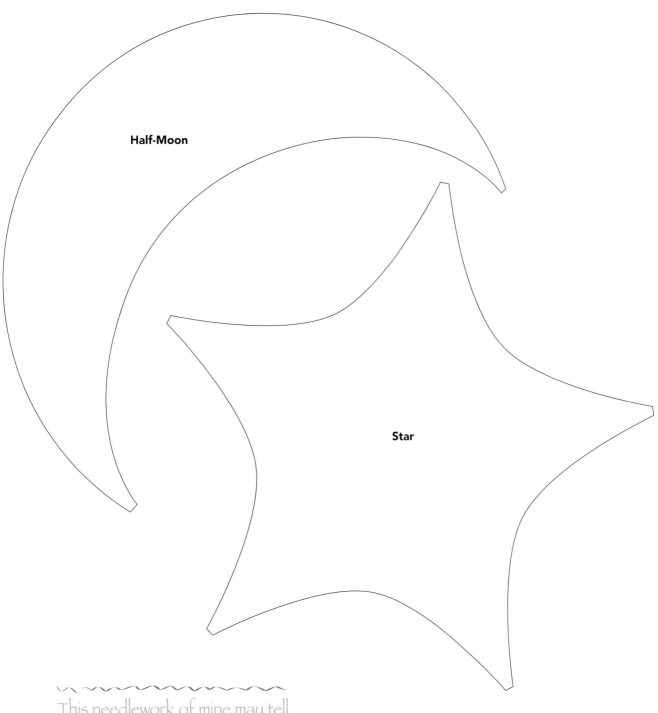

Half-Moon

Star

This needlework of mine may tell
That when a child I learned well
And by my elders I was taught
Not to spend my time for nought.
                    —From an old sampler

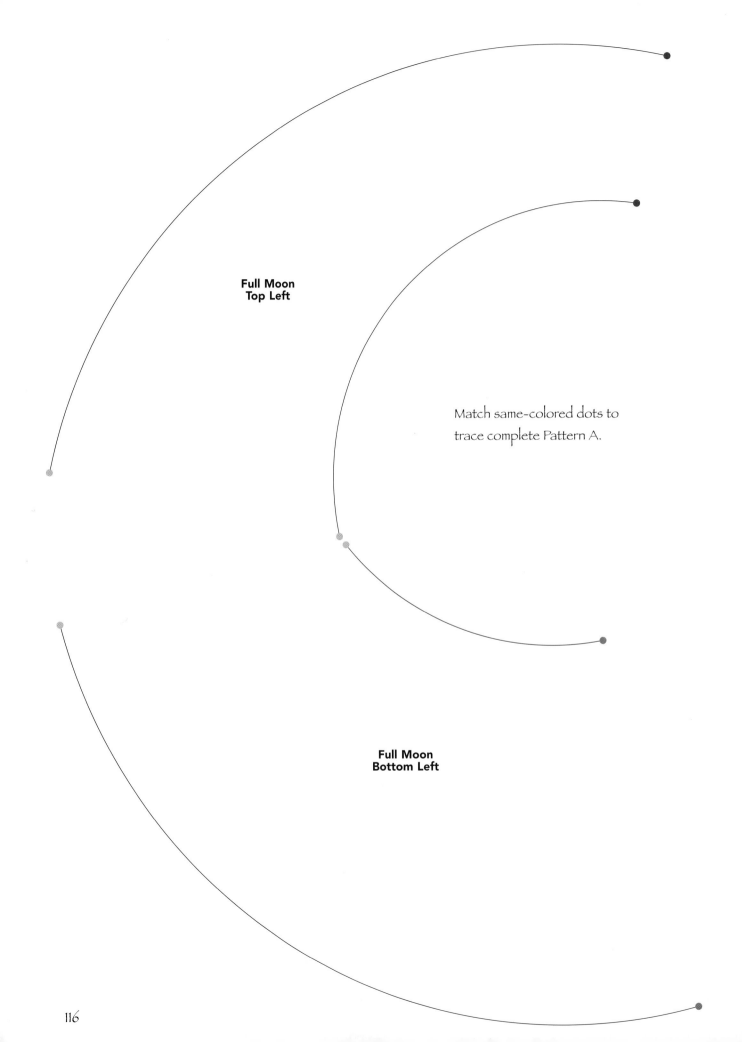

**Full Moon
Top Left**

Match same-colored dots to
trace complete Pattern A.

**Full Moon
Bottom Left**

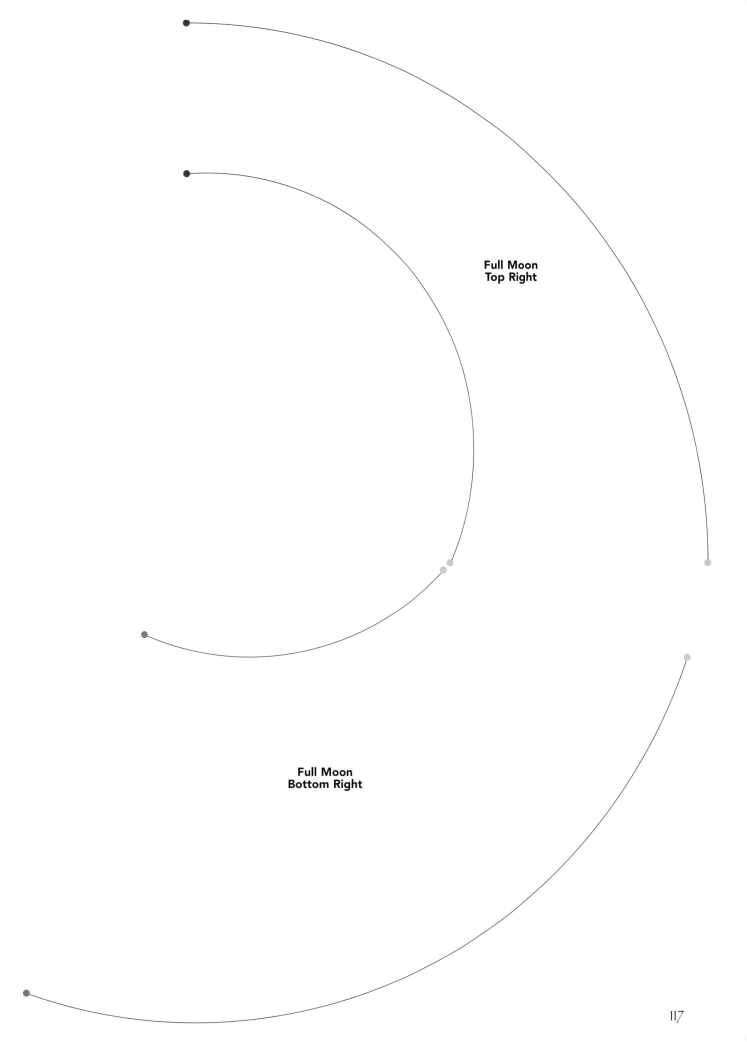

**Full Moon
Top Right**

**Full Moon
Bottom Right**

Plaid Log Cabin

The Log Cabin takes on a bold new look with a twist on tradition. Instead of shading the block half light-half dark, Mary Radke created squares within a square. Using an earth-tone palette of plaids, she created a large, horizontal wall hanging that's a visual playground.

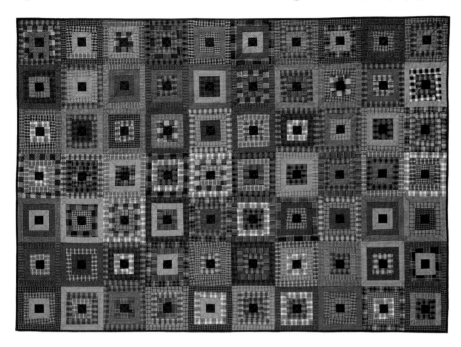

Finished Size: 49" x 70"
Blocks: 70 (7" x 7")

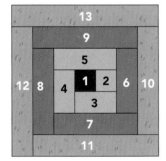

Log Cabin Block—Make 70.

Materials

1 yard black (includes binding)
¼ yard each of 15 plaid fabrics
3 yards backing

Making Blocks

For this stitch-and-cut method, templates are not needed. It is not necessary to cut individual pieces for the logs.

1. Cut a 26" square of black for binding and set aside. From remaining black fabric, cut 7 (1½" x 17") strips. From these, cut 70 (1½") squares for block centers.

2. Cut a 1½"-wide cross-grain strip from each plaid. As you assemble blocks, cut more strips as needed.

3. Select 1 strip for inside "square-within-a-square." From this, cut a 1½" square. Sew square to black center square *(Diagram A)*.

4. Position square pair with plaid square at top; then match same plaid strip to long edge of squares as shown *(Diagram B)*, right sides facing, and stitch. Trim strip even with center square. Press seam allowance toward new log.

5. Turn block to position new log at top. With right sides facing, match same strip to right edge and stitch *(Diagram C)*. Trim log even with block as before and press seam allowance toward new log.

6. Turn unit so newest log is at top. With right sides facing, match same strip to right edge of block and stitch *(Diagram D)*. Trim log even with block and press.

7. Select another strip for middle row. Continue adding logs in same manner. Always sew with last log at top and press toward new log.

8. Repeat with third plaid strip to complete block. Completed block should measure 7½" square.

9. Make 70 Log Cabin blocks. $\longrightarrow$

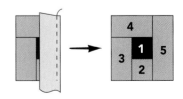

Diagram A

Diagram B

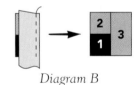

Diagram C

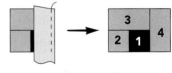

Diagram D

Quilt Assembly

1. Lay out blocks in 7 horizontal rows, with 10 blocks in each row. Arrange blocks to get a pleasing balance of color and value. When satisfied with placement, join blocks in each row.

2. Referring to photo, join rows to complete quilt top.

Quilting and Finishing

1. Mark quilting design on quilt top as desired. Quilt shown has machine-quilted diagonal lines that make an X through each block.

2. Divide backing fabric into 2 equal lengths. See page 135 for instructions on making a backing.

3. Layer backing, batting, and quilt top. Baste. Quilt as desired.

4. Make 7 yards of binding. See page 139 for instructions on making and applying binding.

A Bigger Quilt

It's easy to use these instructions to make a larger quilt. Follow the same steps, but cut 2"-wide squares and strips instead of 1½". The resulting finished blocks will be 10½" square.

Make 72 blocks and set them together in 9 horizontal rows with 8 blocks in each row. The finished quilt will be 84" x 94", ideal for a queen-size bed. Increase yardage of each plaid to ⅜ yard. Yardage for black remains 1 yard, including a 32" square for binding.

No matter how simple or traditional a pattern, the effect of a quilt is still absolutely original because no two people handle fabric and color the same way. —Beth Gutcheon

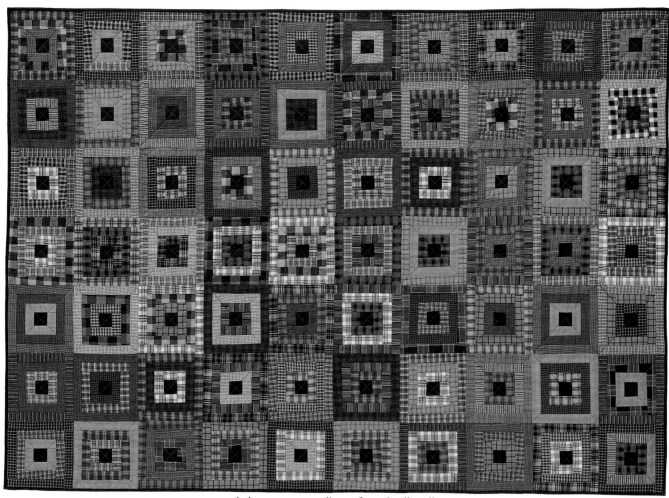

Quilt by Mary Radke of Yorkville, Illinois

Being a beginner is fun if you approach it with a sense of humor. I tell my beginner students about the time my husband gave me golf lessons as a gift. One day, I borrowed a driver and headed for the golf range to practice. When I asked at the desk for a bucket of balls, the woman asked, "Large or small?" Surprised, I replied that I thought the balls only came in one size. "Are we a beginner?" she asked. "I was referring to the size of the bucket!" We both got a big laugh out of it.

With a new endeavor, you have to start somewhere, so just enjoy yourself and don't worry about what you don't know—learning is half the fun. —Lynn Williams Snohomish, Washington

God loves a cheerful ripper.

—Cyndi Wheeler, Birmingham, Alabama

Thanks for Everything
My husband started getting suspicious of how much money I was spending at quilt shops when I started receiving "thank you" notes from them. —Nancy Graves, Manhattan, Kansas

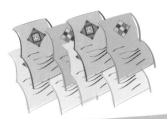

In Stitches
My grandmother's neighbors used to come over for quilting bees until someone discovered that Grandma would pick out their stitches after all the ladies left. Grandma was a kind person and never meant to hurt anybody's feelings. —Lois Vrbka, Fairbanks, Alaska

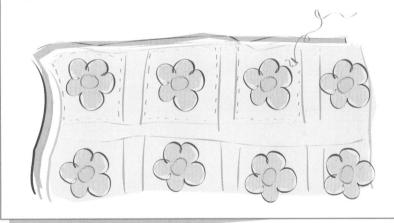

From the Scrap Basket
There is a certain rhythm to hand work that is very soothing. When everything is turned upside down, you can sit down and quilt a few lines and the world is suddenly right side up again . . . your blood pressure is lower, and the only thing that matters is watching the needle and thread move smoothly through the layers of fabric.
　　　　　—Marjean Sargent, Malvern, Iowa

A creative mess is better than tidy idleness.
　　　　　—Laurel Larsen, Cloverdale, California

Someone who makes no mistakes usually doesn't make much of anything. 　　　—Bishop W. C. Magee

Fabric Preparation

Lightweight, 100%-cotton fabric is the best choice for quilts. Sturdy and durable, cotton is neither stretchy nor tightly woven and it takes a crease well, so seams are easy to press. When you use good-quality fabric, your quilt looks nice and lasts a long time.

Selecting Fabric

Choosing fabric seems to bring out insecurities in many quiltmakers. Will my quilt look as good as the one in the picture? If I change the color to blue, will my quilt look as nice as the green one?

Trust Your Instincts. There are no right or wrong choices, nor are there any hard-and-fast rules about fabric selection. Use fabrics you like. You can ask for help from family and friends, but the final choice should be yours.

Work with the staff at your local quilt shop. Take down half the bolts in the store, if necessary, to try different combinations. Group your choices on a table and then—this is very important—step back at least 8 feet and squint. This gives you a preview of the mix of value and texture. If a fabric looks out of place, replace it and try again. And again. And again, until you're satisfied.

Prewashing

Wash, dry, and iron all fabrics before cutting to eliminate the center crease, as well as excess dye and sizing. Also, fabric can shrink slightly after washing. If you take the time to prewash, there's less chance of damage occurring later.

Use the washer and detergent that you'll use to wash the finished quilt. Wash light and dark colors separately in warm water. Use a mild detergent or Orvus

Paste, a mild soap available at many quilt shops.

Test for Colorfastness. Today's improved dyes and processes mean that bleeding is not the problem that it was in your grandmother's time. Nonetheless, you want to be sure to remove excess dye before you use any fabric. If you don't, you risk the fabric bleeding onto another when the finished quilt is washed.

After machine washing the fabric, rinse each piece in the sink, adding a clean scrap of white fabric. If the scrap becomes stained, rinse again with a clean scrap. Continue until the scrap remains white.

If repeated rinsing doesn't stop the bleeding, don't use that fabric—take it back to the store where you bought it and complain!

Dry and Press. Dry prewashed fabrics in the dryer at a medium or permanent-press setting until they're just damp. Then press them dry. It's important to iron out all creases and folds so you'll have smooth, straight fabric with which to work.

Grain Lines

The interwoven lengthwise and crosswise threads of a fabric are grain lines. Think about grain direction before you cut. Cotton fabric can be stable or stretchy, depending on how it is cut.

Selvage. The lengthwise finished edges of the uncut fabric are selvages (*Grain Diagram*). These edges are more tightly woven than the body of the fabric and are sometimes not printed. Always trim selvage from the ends of a strip before cutting pieces for your quilt.

Straight Grain. Lengthwise grain, parallel to the selvage, has the least give. Long strips for sashing and borders, which must retain their shape over time, are best cut lengthwise for stability.

Crosswise grain, perpendicular to the selvage, has more give. For most patchwork pieces, strips are cut on the crosswise grain but either direction is acceptable.

Bias. True bias is at a 45° angle to the selvages, on the diagonal between lengthwise and crosswise grains (*Grain Diagram*). Bias-cut fabric has the most stretch. When you cut a triangle, at least one edge is bias. Handle a bias edge carefully, as it can easily stretch out of shape, warping the patchwork.

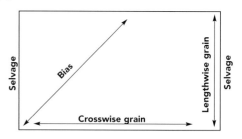

Grain Diagram

Bedcover Size Variations

You might want to change the size of the quilt shown to fit your bed. Consider the quilt's design, the bed's size and style, and your own preferences. Lap quilts, doll quilts, wall hangings, or quilts "just for show" can be any size you like.

Get a Good Fit

The bed style will influence a quilt's finished size. For example, a quilt for a four-poster needs more length and width than one made for a contemporary platform-style bed.

On most beds, a quilt's length and width is affected by whether you use a dust ruffle or let the quilt hang past the box spring, or even to the floor. Also consider the bed's height and whether you want a pillow tuck or to let the quilt lie flat.

Standard Sizes

Once you choose the look you want, refer to the chart below to find the mattress size and the dimensions of the corresponding style of bedcover.

Comforters. Most comforters cover the mattress but not the box spring, nor do they allow for pillow tuck. Treat comforter dimensions as minimum standards if you want to use your quilt with a dust ruffle and decorative pillows.

Bedspreads. A bedspread covers the bed, falls almost to the floor, and allows for a pillow tuck. These sizes are maximum proportions, assuming the top of the mattress is a standard 20" from the floor.

Custom Calculations. The chart gives standard dimensions for four bed sizes. These dimensions include a 12" drop on three sides and 8" for a pillow tuck. If your needs differ, here's how to calculate the best finished size for your quilt.

Start with the mattress dimensions. If you want a pillow tuck, add 8"–10" to the length.

To determine the length of the drop, measure from the top of the mattress to just below the top of the dust ruffle, all the way to the floor, or some desired point in between. For most quilts, you'll add one drop to the length and two drops to the width.

Example. Let's figure the size of a quilt for a queen-size bed. For this example, we'll assume a 12" drop is wanted, but no extra is needed for a pillow tuck.

We know the mattress measures 60" x 80". To figure the quilt width, add 12" twice to the width of mattress: $60" + 12" + 12" = 84"$. To figure the quilt's length, add 12" to the mattress length: $80" + 12" = 92"$.

Finally, remember that the finished size you determine (and the size given with instructions) is a mathematical calculation—the finished size will vary slightly with the effects of sewing and quilting.

Adapting a Design to Fit

If the quilt you plan to make is not the size you want, there are several ways to adapt the design.

To make a smaller quilt, eliminate a row of blocks, set the blocks without sashing, and/or narrow the border widths.

To make a quilt larger, add rows of blocks, sashing, and/or multiple borders. Each addition requires extra yardage, which you should estimate before you buy fabric.

	Standard Mattress Size*	Comforter Size	Bedspread Size	Our Average Quilt Size**
Twin	38" x 75"	58" x 86"	80" x 108"	62" x 95"
Full	53" x 75"	73" x 86"	96" x 108"	77" x 95"
Queen	60" x 80"	80" x 88"	102" x 118"	84" x 100"
King	76" x 80"	96" x 88"	120" x 118"	100" x 100"

*Standards for spring mattresses; waterbeds may vary.
**Includes 12" drop at end and sides, as well as 8" for pillow tuck.

Rotary Cutting

Rotary cutting is fast and easy. It's fast because you measure and cut with one stroke, skipping steps of making templates and marking fabric. It's accurate because the fabric stays flat as you cut, instead of being raised by a scissor blade. If rotary cutting is new to you, use these instructions to practice on scraps. Rotary cutting may seem strange at first, but give it a try—you'll love it!

Rotary cutting often begins with cutting fabric strips which are then cut into smaller pieces. Unless specified otherwise, cut strips crosswise, selvage to selvage. Instructions specify the number and width of strips needed, as well as the size and quantity of pieces to cut from these strips. *Seam allowances are included in measurements given for all strips and pieces.*

A rotary cutter is fun to use, but it is very sharp and should be handled with caution. Carelessness can result in cutting yourself, other people, or objects that you had no intention of slicing. Always keep the safety guard in place on the cutter until you're ready to use it. In use or in storage, keep the cutter out of reach of children.

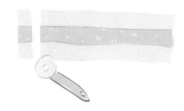

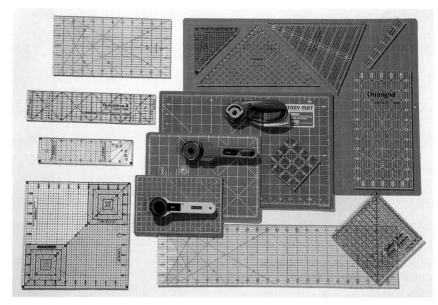

1. Cutters, mats, and rulers come in many sizes and styles. Choose a cutter that is comfortable to hold. Change the blade when it becomes dull. The most useful cutting mat is 24" x 36", but you may want a smaller one for cutting scraps.

Rotary-cutting rulers are made of thick, transparent acrylic. Select rulers that are marked in increments of 1", ¼", and ⅛". A 45°-angle line is also useful. Rulers are available in many sizes and shapes. The most popular rulers are a 6" x 24" for cutting long strips, a 15" square, and a 6" x 12" for small cuts.

2. To cut straight strips, you must square up an edge. Start by folding the fabric in half, matching selvages. Fold again, aligning the selvage with the first fold to make four layers. Let the yardage extend to the right, leaving the end to be cut on the mat. (Reverse directions if you are left-handed.)

3. Align one edge of a large square ruler with the bottom fold. The left edge of the square should be about 1" from the rough edge of the fabric. Butt a long ruler against the left side of the square, overlapping top and bottom fabric edges. Carefully remove the square, keeping the long ruler in place.

4. Holding the long ruler still with your left hand, place the cutter blade against the ruler at the bottom of the mat. Begin rolling the cutter before it meets the fabric, moving it away from you. Use firm, even pressure, keeping the ruler stable and the blade against the ruler. Do not lift the cutter until it cuts through the opposite edge of the fabric.

5. To measure the strip width, place the ruler on the left edge of the fabric. Carefully align the desired measurement on the ruler with the fabric, checking the ruler line from top to bottom of the fabric. Cut, holding the ruler firmly in place. A sharp blade cuts easily through four layers.

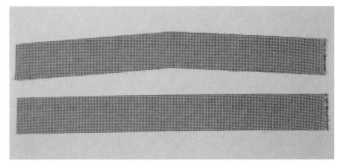

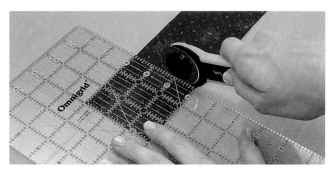

6. Check the cut strip. If the fabric edge is not squared up properly, the strip will bow in the middle (top). If necessary, square up the edge again and cut another strip. When satisfied with cut strips, rotary-cut ½" from the strip ends to remove the selvages.

7. To cut squares and rectangles from a strip, align the desired measurement on the ruler with the end of the strip. Check ruler alignment from top to bottom and from side to side to be sure the ruler is straight. When satisfied, cut.

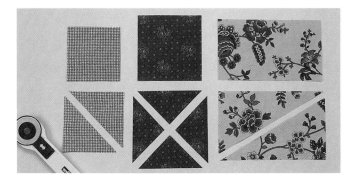

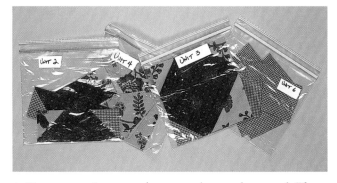

8. For right triangles, instructions may say to cut a square in half or in quarters diagonally. This works with rectangles, too. The edges of the square or the rectangle are straight grain, so the triangle's diagonal edges, from the inside of the square, are bias. Handle these bias edges as little as possible and with care to keep the fabric from stretching as you work with it.

9. Keep cut pieces and sewn units neatly stored. If you constantly move your work on and off the dining room table, it's easy to get pieces mixed up. Store cut pieces in zip-top plastic bags labeled with the appropriate unit number. If the sewing takes several weeks, your pieces won't get lost, mixed up, or dirty. Remove one piece at a time as you work.

Cutting with Templates

A template is a duplication of a printed pattern that you use to trace a shape onto fabric. Use templates to accurately mark curves and complex shapes. For straight-sided shapes, it is a matter of preference whether you use templates or a rotary cutter and ruler.

Oxmoor House patterns are full-size. Patterns for pieced blocks show the seam line (dashed) and the cutting line (solid). Appliqué patterns do not include seam allowances. To make a template from dimensions given for rotary cutting, use a ruler to draw a pattern onto template material.

We recommend template plastic, which is easy to cut and can be used repeatedly without fraying or cracking. Best of all, the transparency of the plastic allows you to trace a pattern directly onto it. Templates made of this plastic are more reliable than those cut from cardboard or sandpaper.

To check the accuracy of your templates, cut and piece a test block before cutting more pieces.

1. Trace the pattern onto plastic, using a ruler to draw straight lines. If desired, punch ⅛"-diameter holes at the corners of the template's seam line to enable you to mark pivot points.

2. For piecing, place the template facedown on the wrong side of the fabric and trace around the shape. Use common lines for efficient cutting.

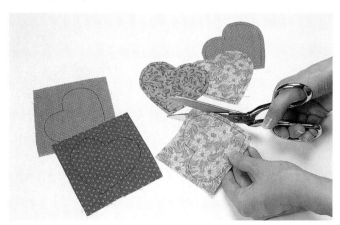

3. For appliqué, trace template on right side of fabric. (A lightly drawn line disappears into the fold of the seam allowance when the piece is stitched to the background fabric.) Position tracings at least ½" apart so you can add seam allowances when cutting each piece.

4. A window template provides the guidance of a drawn seam line, which is very useful for sewing a set-in seam. When traced on the right side of the fabric, a window template can help you to center specific motifs with accuracy.

Machine-Piecing Basics

A consistent ¼" seam allowance is essential for accurate piecing. If each seam varies by the tiniest bit, the difference multiplies greatly by the time a block is complete. Be sure you can sew a precise ¼" seam allowance.

On some sewing machines, you can position the needle to sew a ¼" seam. Or use a presser foot that measures ¼" from the needle to the outside edge of the foot. These feet are available at sewing supply stores. If neither option is available, make a seam guide as described under Photo 1.

To test your seam allowance, cut three 1½" fabric squares and join them in a row. Press the seams and measure—if the strip is not precisely 3½", try again with a deeper or shallower seam allowance.

Set your sewing machine to 12–14 stitches per inch. Use 100% cotton or cotton/polyester sewing thread.

With right sides facing, sew each seam from cut edge to cut edge of the fabric. It is not necessary to backstitch, because most seams are crossed and held by another.

The following are other points that will make machine piecing easy.

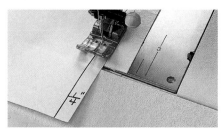

1. Use a ruler and a sharp pencil to draw a line ¼" from the edge of a piece of paper. Lower the machine needle onto the line, drop the foot, and adjust the paper to parallel the foot. Lay masking tape on the plate at the edge of the paper. Sew a test seam. If seam allowances get wider or narrower, the tape is not straight.

2. When you piece triangles with other units, seams should cross in an X on the back. When these units are joined, the joining seam should go precisely through the center of the X so the triangle will have a nice sharp point on the front.

3. To press, use an up-and-down motion. (Sliding the iron can push seams out of shape.) Press the seam on the wrong side. On the right side, press seam allowances to one side, not open as in dressmaking. Press seam allowances so they will offset where seams meet. If possible, press toward a dark fabric.

4. Use pins to match seam lines. With right sides facing, align opposing seams, nesting seam allowances. On the top piece, push a pin through the seam line ¼" from the edge. Then push the pin through the bottom seam and set it. Pin all matching seams; then stitch the joining seam, removing pins as you sew.

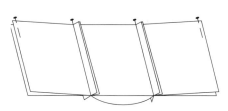

5. Sometimes two units that should match are slightly different. To join these units, pin-match seams and sew with the shorter piece on top. The feed dogs ease the fullness on the bottom piece. If units are too different to ease, resew the one that varies most from the desired size.

6. Chain piecing is an efficient way to sew many units in one operation. Sew one unit as usual, but at the end of the seam do not clip the thread or lift the foot. Instead, feed in the next unit on the heels of the first, assembly-line style. Sew as many seams as you like on a chain. Clip threads as you press.

Quick-Piecing Techniques

The methods described here are uniquely suited to machine sewing. Combined with rotary cutting, they reduce cutting and sewing time without sacrificing results. Before starting your quilt project, practice a required technique that is new to you. You'll love how fast and easy the pieces come together!

Diagonal Corners turn squares into sewn triangles with just a stitch and a snip. This technique is particularly helpful if the corner triangle is very small, because it's easier to cut and handle a square than a small triangle. By sewing squares to squares, you don't have to guess where seam allowances meet, which can be difficult with triangles.

Project instructions give the size of the fabric pieces needed. The base fabric is either a square or a rectangle, but the contrasting corner always starts out as a square.

Diagonal Ends are sewn in a similar manner as diagonal corners. This method joins two rectangles on the diagonal without your having to measure and cut a trapezoid. Project instructions specify the size of each rectangle. To sew diagonal ends, make a seam guide for your sewing machine as described in Step 1 for diagonal corners.

Strip Piecing requires you to join strips of different fabrics to make a strip set. From these, you cut segments that become units of patchwork. Project directions specify how to cut strips and each strip set is illustrated. This is a fast and accurate technique because you sew and press the strip set before you cut individual units.

Diagonal Corners

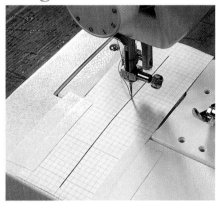

1. Make a seam guide that will help you sew diagonal lines without having to mark the fabric beforehand. Draw a line on paper. Lower the needle onto the line. (Remove the foot if necessary for a good viewpoint.) Use a ruler to confirm that the line is parallel to the needle. Tape the paper in place; then trim it as needed to clear the needle and feed dogs.

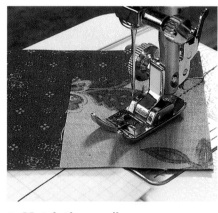

2. Match the small square to one corner of the base fabric, right sides facing. Align the top tip of the small square with the needle and the bottom tip with the seam guide. Stitch a diagonal seam from tip to tip, keeping the bottom tip of the small square in line with the seam guide.

3. Press the small square in half at the seam.

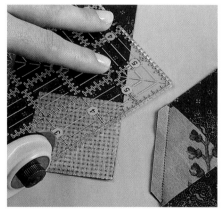

4. Trim the seam allowance to ¼". Repeat the procedure to add a corner to two, three, or four corners of the base fabric. The technique is the same when you add a diagonal corner to a strip set—treat the base fabric as one piece, even if it is already pieced.

Diagonal Ends

1. Position rectangles perpendicular to each other with right sides facing, matching corners to be sewn. Before you sew, pin on the stitching line and check the right side to see if the line is angled in the desired direction. (It's easy to get mixed up and sew in the wrong direction!)

Position rectangles under the needle, leading with the top edge. Sew a diagonal seam to the opposite edge.

2. Check the right side to see that the seam is angled correctly. Then press the seam and trim excess fabric from the seam allowance.

As noted in Step 1, the direction of the seam makes a difference. Make mirror-image units with this in mind, or you can put different ends on the same strip.

Strip Piecing

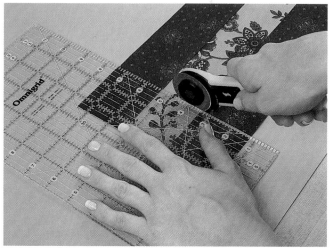

1. To sew a strip set, match each pair of strips with right sides facing. Sew through both layers along one long edge. As you add strips to the set, sew each new seam in the opposite direction from the last one. This distributes tension evenly in both directions and keeps the strip set from getting warped and wobbly.

2. When a strip set is assembled and pressed, you will be directed to cut it into segments. Use a ruler to measure; then make appropriate crosswise cuts to get individual segments.

Quick-Pieced Triangle-Squares

Many patchwork designs are made by joining contrasting triangles to make triangle-squares. These can consist of two or four contrasting right triangles.

Cutting and sewing triangles pose unique problems for quilters. These quick-piecing techniques eliminate those difficulties and enable you to create many pre-sewn units with one process—a real time-saver.

These instructions use a grid method. A grid is marked on the fabric and then stitched as described below.

Cutting instructions specify two fabric pieces for each grid. We recommend that you spray both pieces with spray starch to keep the fabric from distorting during marking and stitching. For marking, use a see-through ruler and a fine-tipped fabric pen—a pencil drags on the fabric, making an inaccurate line and stretching the fabric. Accuracy is important in every step—if your marking, cutting, sewing, and pressing are not precise, your triangle-squares may be lopsided or the wrong size.

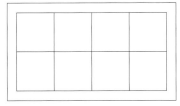

1. For our example, let's say instructions call for a 2 x 4 grid of 2⅞" squares. This describes a grid of eight squares, drawn two down and four across. Draw the grid on the wrong side of the lighter fabric. The fabric size specified allows a margin of at least 1" around the grid, so align the ruler parallel to one long edge of the fabric, 1" from the edge, and draw the first line.

Draw the second line exactly 2⅞" below the first. Use the ruler's markings to position each new line. Take care to make lines accurately parallel and/or perpendicular.

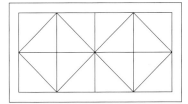

2. When the grid is completely drawn, draw a diagonal line through each square. Alternate direction of diagonals in adjacent squares, as shown above.

In this example, we're working toward a desired finished size of 2" square. The grid squares are drawn ⅞" larger than the finished size. After the grid is sewn, the cut and pressed square is ½" larger than the finished size (2½").

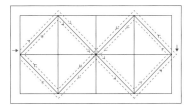

3. With right sides facing, match edges of the two fabric pieces. Start at a corner of the grid (blue arrow). Stitch a ¼" seam allowance along the diagonals indicated by the blue line. At the end of a line, sew into the margin as shown. Keep the needle down, raise the foot, and pivot the fabric to sew the next line. When you return to the start, you'll have sewn one side of all diagonal lines.

Begin again at another point (red arrow). Repeat stitching on the opposite side of the diagonal lines. When the grid is completely stitched, press the fabric to smooth the stitching.

4. Rotary-cut on all the drawn lines to separate the triangle-squares. Each grid square yields two triangle-squares, so our example will produce 16 units.

5. Press each triangle-square open, pressing the seam allowance toward the darker fabric. Trim points from ends of each seam allowance.

Traditional Appliqué

Appliqué is the process of sewing pieces onto a background to create a fabric picture. The edges of appliqué pieces are turned under and sewn to the background by hand or by machine.

For hand appliqué, the edges of each piece must be turned under by hand. You can avoid this with some machine techniques. Usually, however, machine appliqué is accomplished by preparing pieces in the same manner and using a topstitch or blindhem stitch to secure them to the background.

For traditional hand appliqué, follow steps 1–2 at right. See page 126, Step 3, for tips on making templates and cutting appliqué pieces. Some quilters find it easier to turn edges with freezer-paper templates as described below.

1. For traditional hand appliqué, use the drawn line as a guide to turn under seam allowances on each piece. Do not turn an edge that will be covered by another piece. Hand-baste seam allowances. (You can eliminate basting, if you prefer, and rely on rolling the edge under with the tip of your needle as you sew. This is called needle-turned appliqué.) Pin appliqué pieces to the background fabric.

2. Slipstitch around each piece, using thread that matches the appliqué. (We used contrasting thread for photography.) Pull the needle through the background and catch a few threads on the fold of the appliqué. Reinsert the needle into the background and bring the needle up through the appliqué for the next stitch. Make close, tiny stitches that do not show on the right side. Remove basting.

Freezer-Paper Appliqué

Usually, you'll trace a full-size pattern onto the dull side of freezer paper. When working with freezer paper, the finished appliqué is a mirror image of the pattern. So, if the pattern is an irregular shape (not symmetrical), first make a tracing-paper pattern so you can turn it over when you trace the shape onto freezer paper and prevent the appliqué from being reversed. Cut out each freezer-paper template on the drawn lines.

Use a dry iron at wool setting to press shiny side of paper template to wrong side of fabric. Allow at least ½" between templates for seam allowances.

1. Cut out appliqué pieces, adding ¼" seam allowance around each shape. With small, sharp scissors, snip seam allowance at curves, clipping halfway to paper edge. This allows the seam allowance to spread when turned so curve will lie flat.

2. Apply fabric glue to wrong side of each seam allowance. Use your fingers or a cool, dry iron to turn the seam allowances over the template edges where the glue will secure them to the paper. Do not turn an edge that will be covered by another piece. Pin and sew pieces in place as described in steps 1 and 2 above.

3. When stitching is complete, turn the work to the wrong side. Trim background fabric behind the appliqué, leaving scant ¼" seam allowances. Moisten the fabric with a spray of water to dissolve the glue. Use tweezers to remove the paper pieces.

Joining Blocks

The easiest way to join blocks is in rows, either vertically, horizontally, or diagonally.

Arrange blocks and setting pieces, if any, on the floor or a large table. Identify the pieces in each row and verify the position of each block. This is playtime—moving the blocks around to find the best balance of color and value is great fun. Don't start sewing until you're happy with the placement of each block.

As you join blocks in each row, pick up one block at a time to avoid confusion. Pin-match adjoining seams. Re-press a seam if necessary to offset seam allowances. If you find some blocks are larger than others, pinning may help determine where easing is required. A blast of steam from the iron may help fit the blocks together.

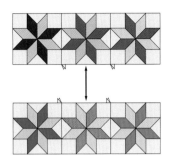

1. Press seam allowances between blocks in the same direction. From row to row, press in opposite directions so that seam allowances will offset when rows are joined.

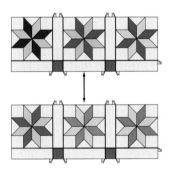

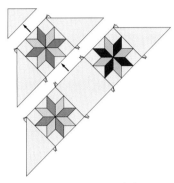

2. In an alternate set, straight or diagonal, press seam allowances between blocks toward setting squares or triangles. This creates the least bulk and always results in opposing seam allowances when adjacent rows are joined.

3. Sashing eliminates questions about pressing. Just remember to always press toward the sashing. Assemble rows with sashing strips between blocks, pressing each new seam allowance toward the sashing. If necessary, ease the block to match the strip. Assemble the quilt with sashing rows between block rows.

Borders

Most quilts have one or more borders that frame the central design. Borders can be plain, pieced, or appliquéd; corners are square or mitered.

Colors, shapes, and proportions of border pieces should complement those in the quilt. The color of an outside border makes that color dominant in the quilt. For example, if a quilt has equal amounts of red, white, and blue, a red border brings out the red in the pieced design.

Measuring

It's common for one side of a sewn quilt to be a slightly different measurement than its opposite side. Little variables in cutting and piecing just add up. Sewing borders of equal length to opposite sides will square up the quilt.

Most cutting instructions include extra length for border strips to allow for piecing variations. Before sewing them, trim border strips to fit your quilt properly. How you measure, trim, and sew border strips depends on the type of corner you're making.

Square Corners. Measure from top to bottom through the middle of the quilt (*Diagram 1*). Trim side borders to this length and sew them to the quilt sides. You may need to ease one side of a quilt to fit the border and then stretch the opposite side to fit the same border length. In the end, both sides will be the same.

For top and bottom borders, measure from side to side through the middle of the quilt, including side borders and seam allowances. Trim remaining borders to this length and sew them to the quilt.

Mitered Corners. The seam of a mitered corner is more subtle than that of a square corner, so it creates the illusion of a continuous line around the quilt. Mitered corners are particularly suitable for borders of striped fabric, pieced borders, or multiple plain borders. Multiple borders should be sewn together and the resulting striped unit treated as a single border for mitering.

Measure the quilt's length through the middle *(Diagram 2)*. Subtract ½" for seam allowances at the outer edges. Mark the center of each border strip. Working out from the center, measure and mark the determined length on the border strip.

Measure the quilt's width and repeat marking on remaining border strips. Do not trim borders until after corner seam is sewn.

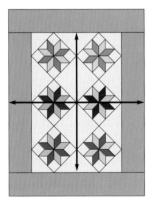

Diagram 1

Diagram 2

Sewing a Mitered Corner

1. On the wrong side of each edge of the quilt, mark the center and each corner, ¼" from the edge. These marks correspond to marks on each border strip. Pin borders to quilt with right sides together, matching marked points.

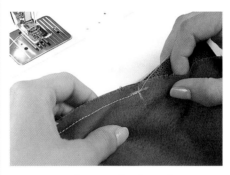

2. Backstitching at both ends, sew the border seam from match point to match point, easing as needed. Join remaining borders in the same manner. (We've used contrasting thread for photography.)

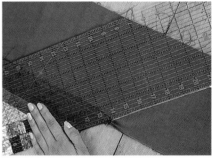

3. Fold the quilt at one corner to align adjacent borders, right sides together. Align ruler with the fold of the quilt. Along the edge of the ruler (which is at a 45° angle to the border), draw a line from the corner of the seam to the outside edge. This is the sewing line for the miter.

4. Beginning with a backstitch at the corner, stitch on the marked line to the outside edge. Check the right side to see that the seam is flat and stripes match. When satisfied with seam, trim fabric to a ¼" seam allowance.

5. Press mitered seam open or to one side, as you prefer, so that the interior portion of the quilt lies flat. Then press the seam on the right side of the quilt.

Marking a Quilting Design

The quilting design is an important part of any quilt, so choose it with care. The hours you spend stitching together the layers of your quilt create shadows and depths that bring the quilt to life, so make the design count.

Most quilters mark a quilting design on the quilt top before it is layered and basted. To do this, you need marking pencils, a long ruler or yardstick, stencils for quilting motifs, and a smooth, hard surface on which to work. Press the quilt top thoroughly before you begin.

To find a stencil for a quilting design, check your local quilt shop or mail-order catalogs for one that suits your quilt. Or, if you know what kind of design you want, make your own stencil.

Test Markers

Before using any marker, test it on scraps to be sure marks will wash out. Don't use just any pencil because that's what your grandmother used. There are many pencils and chalk markers available that are designed to wash out. No matter what marking tool you use, lightly drawn lines are easier to remove than heavy ones.

Marking a Grid

Many quilts feature a grid of squares or diamonds as a quilting design in the background areas of the quilt. Use a ruler to mark a grid, starting at one border seam and working toward the opposite edge. Mark parallel lines, spacing them as desired (usually 1" apart), until background areas are marked as desired.

Stencils

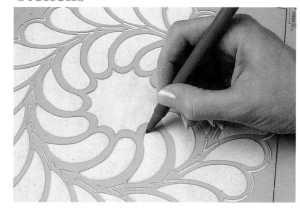

1. To transfer a design to the quilt top, position the stencil on the quilt and mark through the slits in the stencil. Connect the lines after removing the stencil.

2. To make a stencil, trace a design onto freezer paper or template plastic. Use a craft knife to cut little slots along the lines of the design. Place the stencil on the right side of the fabric and mark in each slot.

Quilting Without Marking

Some quilts are quilted in-the-ditch (right in the seams) or outline-quilted (¼" from the seam line). These methods do not require marking.

If you are machine quilting, use the edge of your presser foot and the seam line as guides for outline quilting. If you are hand quilting, use narrow drafting tape as a guideline between the seam and the quilting line.

Another option is stippling—freestyle, meandering lines of quilting worked closely together to fill open areas. This can be done by hand or by machine, letting your needle go where the mood takes you.

Making a Backing

Use the same quality of fabric for your backing as for the top. The fabric can match the top, or you can piece scraps to make a back that is as creative as the top.

The backing should be at least 3" larger than the quilt top on all sides. For quilts up to 40" wide, use one length of 45"-wide cotton fabric. For a large quilt, 90"- or 108"-wide fabric is a sensible option that reduces waste and eliminates backing seams. But selection is limited in wide fabrics, so many quilters piece two or three lengths of 45"-wide fabric to make a backing.

Choose a light backing fabric for light-colored quilts, because you don't want a dark color to show through. To show off your stitching, select a plain fabric. If you don't want to showcase your quilting this way, choose a busy print for the backing as camouflage or piece the backing from assorted scraps.

Most quilt backs have two or three seams (*Backing Options Diagram*) to avoid having a seam in the center back. (Many experts feel that a center seam augments the creases formed by routine folding of a quilt.) Press seam allowances open.

Backing Options Diagram

A scrappy backing is a good way to use up old or leftover fabrics—and make the back almost as much fun as the top. This is how Marion Watchinski got creative with the back of Moon & Stars Whimsy *(page 112).*

Batting

When selecting batting, consider loft, washability, and fiber content. Read the package label to decide if a particular product suits your needs.

Precut batting comes in five sizes. The precut batt listed for each quilt is the most suitable for the quilt's finished size. Some stores sell 90"-wide batting by the yard, which might be more practical for your quilt.

Loft. Loft is the height or thickness of the batting. For a traditional flat look, choose low-loft cotton batting. Polyester batting is available in medium and low lofts that are suitable for most quilts. Thick batting is difficult to quilt, but it's nice for a puffy tied comforter.

Cotton. Cotton batting provides the flat, thin look of an antique quilt. Cotton shrinks slightly when washed, giving it that wrinkled look characteristic of old quilts, so always wash quilts with cotton batting in cold water to prevent excessive shrinking. Most cotton batting should be closely quilted, with quilting lines no more than 1" apart.

Polyester. Look for the word "bonded" when selecting polyester batting. Bonding keeps the loft of the batt uniform and reduces the effects of bearding (the migration of loose fibers through the quilt top). Polyester batting is easy to stitch and can be machine washed with little shrinkage. Avoid bonded batts that feel stiff.

Fleece and Flannel. Fleece is the thinnest of all low-loft batts. It is recommended for use in clothing, table runners, or wall hangings. A single layer of prewashed cotton flannel is good for tablecloths.

Layering

A quilt is a three-layer sandwich held together with quilting stitches. Before you layer the quilt top on the batting and backing, unfold the batting and let it "relax" for a few hours.

Lay backing right side down on a large work surface—a large table, two tables pushed together, or a clean floor. Use masking tape to secure the edges, keeping the backing wrinkle-free and slightly taut.

Smooth the batting over the backing; then trim batting even with the backing. Center the pressed quilt top right side up on the batting. Make sure edges of backing and quilt top are parallel.

Basting

Basting keeps layers from shifting during quilting. Baste with a long needle and white thread. Or use safety pins, if you prefer.

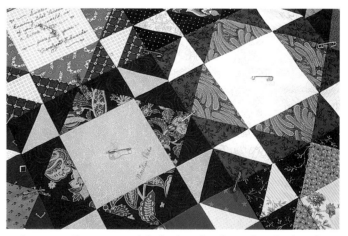

1. Start in the center and baste a line of stitches to each corner, making a large X. Use white thread; colored thread can leave residue on light fabrics. Then baste parallel lines 6"–8" apart. Finish with a line of basting ¼" from each edge of the quilt.

2. Some quilters use nickel-plated safety pins for basting. Pin every 2"–3". Don't close the pins as you go, which can pucker the backing. When all pins are in place, remove the tape at the quilt edges. Gently tug the backing as you close each pin so that pleats don't form underneath.

Quilting

Quilting is the process of stitching the layers of a quilt together, by hand or by machine. The choice of hand or machine quilting depends on the design of the quilt, its intended use, and how much time you want to devote to quilting. The techniques differ, but the results of both are functional and attractive.

Hand Quilting

To quilt by hand, you need a quilting hoop or a frame, quilting thread (which is heavier than sewing thread), quilting needles, and a thimble. If you're not used to a thimble, you'll find it necessary to prevent the needle from digging into your finger.

Preparation. Put the basted quilt in a hoop or frame. Start with a size 7 or 8 "between," or quilting needle. (As your skill increases, try a shorter between to make smaller stitches. A higher number indicates a shorter needle.) Thread the needle with 18" of quilting thread and make a small knot in the end.

The Stitch. Quilting is a running stitch that goes through all three layers of the quilt. Stitches should be small (8–10 per inch), straight, and evenly spaced. Uniformity is more important than length. Don't worry if you take only 5–6 stitches per inch—concentrate on even and straight; tiny comes with practice.

Pop the Knot. Insert the needle through the top about 1" from the point where the quilting will start. Slide the needle through the batting, without piercing the backing, and pull it out where the first stitch will be. Pull the thread taut and tug gently until the knot pops through the top and lodges in the batting (*Knot Diagram*). If it does not pop through, use your needle to gently separate the fabric threads to let the knot through.

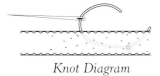

Knot Diagram

Machine Quilting

Choose a small project for your first try at machine quilting, because the bulk of a large quilt can be difficult to manage. Plan simple quilting with continuous straight lines. Good choices are outline or in-the-ditch quilting and allover grids. When you are comfortable with machine quilting, try free-motion quilting and more complex designs.

Preparation. For quilting straight lines, use an even-feed presser foot or a walking foot. You can machine-quilt without this foot, but the work is much easier with it.

Thread the machine with .004 monofilament "invisible" thread or regular sewing thread in a color that coordinates with the quilt. For the bobbin, use sewing thread that matches the backing. Set the stitch length at 8–10 stitches per inch. Adjust the tension so that the bobbin thread does not pull to the top.

Roll the sides of the quilt to the middle and secure the rolls with clips. If you're working on a large quilt, extend your work area by setting up tables to the left and behind the machine to support the quilt while you work.

Straight Lines. Work in long, continuous lines as much as possible. The block seam lines form a grid of long lines across the quilt— quilt these first, starting at the top center and stitching to the opposite edge. Quilt the next line from bottom to top. Alternating the direction of quilting lines keeps the layers from shifting.

$\longrightarrow$

Tying

Tying is a fast and easy way to secure the quilt layers. It's the best way to work with thick batting for puffy comforters. Tying is also fine for polyester batting, but not for cotton or silk batts, which require close quilting.

For ties, use pearl cotton, lightweight yarn, floss, or narrow ribbon; these are stable enough to stay tightly tied. You'll also need a sharp needle with an eye large enough to accommodate the tie material.

Thread the needle with 6" of thread or yarn. Do not knot the ends. Starting in the center of your basted quilt top, take a small stitch through all three layers. Center a 3"-long tail on each side of the stitch (*Diagram 1*). Tie the tails in a tight double knot (*Diagram 2*). Make a tie at least every 6" across the surface of the quilt. Trim the tails of all knots to a uniform length.

Bind the quilt as described on pages 139 and 140. If your quilt has thick batting, you'll want to cut wider binding strips.

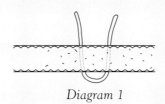

Diagram 1

Diagram 2

Hand Quilting

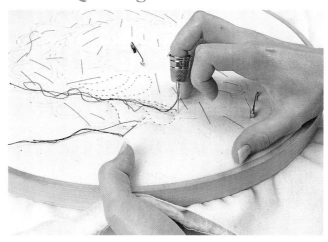

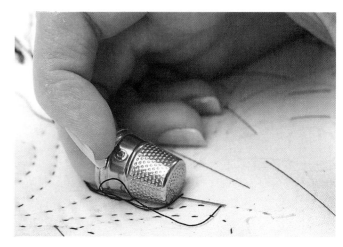

1. To make a stitch, first insert the needle straight down. With your other hand under the quilt, feel for the needle point as it pierces the backing. With practice, you'll be able to find the point without pricking your finger.

2. Roll the needle to a nearly horizontal position. Use the thumb of your sewing hand and the underneath hand to pinch a little hill in the fabric as you push the needle back through the quilt top. Then rock the needle back to an upright position for the next stitch. Load 3–4 stitches on the needle before pulling it through.

With 6" of thread left, tie a knot close to the quilt top. Backstitch; then pop the knot into the batting. Run the thread through the batting and out the top to clip it.

Machine Quilting

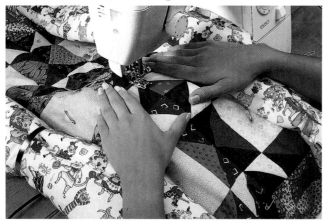

1. Use your hands to spread the fabric slightly. Gently push the quilt toward the foot to reduce the drag on the fabric. Quilt vertical lines on half the quilt, unrolling it until you reach the edge. Remove the quilt from the machine and reroll it so you can quilt the other half. When all vertical lines are done, reroll the quilt in the other direction to quilt horizontal lines in the same manner.

2. Following a curved design is a skill that takes practice and patience to master. Start with a small project that is easy to handle. Attach a darning foot or free-motion quilting foot to your machine. Lower the feed dogs or cover them. You control the stitch length by manually moving the fabric.

Place your hands on each side of the foot so you can maneuver the fabric. To make even stitches, run the machine at a slow, steady speed. Move the fabric smoothly and evenly so that the needle follows the design. Do not rotate the quilt; simply move it forward, backward, and side to side.

Binding

These instructions are for double-fold binding. Doubled binding is stronger than one layer, so it better protects the edges, which get the most wear.

Cut strips 2"–2½" wide to make a finished binding ⅜"–½" wide. Cut wider binding strips when using a thick batting.

Whether to make bias or straight-grain binding is a personal choice. With bias, woven threads crisscross and reinforce the quilt edge. With straight-grain, single threads run parallel to the edge, making a weaker binding. But straight-grain is generally easier to make and often requires less fabric. If you make double-fold binding, straight-grain strips are usually satisfactory.

See steps 1–5 to make continuous bias or Step 6 for joining straight-grain strips. To prepare and apply binding, follow steps 7–14.

1. To cut bias binding, start with a square. (For a queen-size quilt, a 32" square is sufficient.) Center pins at top and bottom edges with their heads toward the inside. At each side, center a pin with the head toward the outside edge. Cut the square in half diagonally to get two triangles.

2. With right sides facing, match edges with pin heads pointed to the outside. Remove pins and join triangles with a ¼" seam. Press the seam open.

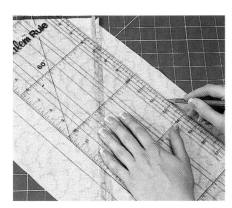

3. On the wrong side of the fabric, mark cutting lines parallel to the long edges. Space between lines should be the width of the binding strip desired. For a 2"-wide binding strip, draw lines 2" apart.

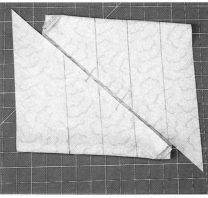

4. Match edges with pin heads pointed to the inside, right sides facing, offsetting one width of binding strip as shown. Join edges with a ¼" seam to make a tube. Press the seam open.

5. Begin cutting at the extended edge. Follow the drawn lines, rolling the tube around as you cut, until all the fabric is cut in a continuous strip. $\longrightarrow$

6. For straight-grain binding, cut crossgrain strips. Lay two strips perpendicular to each other, right sides facing; then sew a diagonal seam across the corner. Trim seam allowances and press them open. Make a continuous strip that is the length needed for the project.

7. Press the strip in half along the length of the strip, wrong sides facing.

8. With edges aligned, position the binding on the front of the quilt top, in the middle of any side. Leave about 3" of binding free before the point where you begin.

9. Stitch through all layers with a ¼" seam. Stop stitching ¼" from the quilt corner and backstitch. (Placing a pin at the ¼" point beforehand will show you where to stop.) Remove the quilt from the machine.

10. Rotate the quilt a quarter turn. Fold the binding straight up, away from the corner, to make a 45°-angle fold.

11. Fold the binding straight down in line with the next edge, leaving the top fold even with the raw edge of the previously sewn side. Begin stitching ¼" from the edge, sewing through all layers. Stitch all corners in this manner. Stop stitching about 4" before the starting point. Choose Step 12 or Step 13 (a and b) to finish.

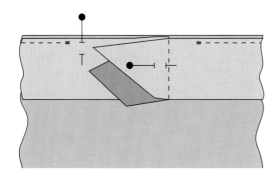

12. Bring both ends of binding together, right sides facing. Where they meet at the quilt surface, hand-baste a seam. Check to see that the seam lies flat, then machine-stitch. Trim seam allowances to ¼" and press open. Stitch unsewn edge of binding to quilt. Go to Step 14; steps 13a and 13b are an alternative method.

13a. Fold beginning 3" tail of binding over on itself and pin. Then sew the binding end over it, overlapping the folded section. Continue stitching through all layers to 1" beyond the folded tail. Trim extra binding.

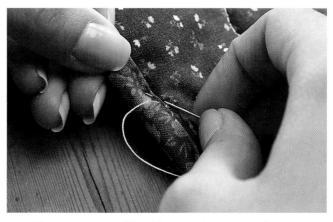

13b. The beginning fold conceals the raw end of the binding when it is turned over to the back side.

14. Trim batting and backing nearly even with seam allowance, leaving a little extra to fill out the binding.
Fold the binding over the seam allowance to the back. Blindstitch folded edge of binding to the backing fabric. Fold a miter into the binding at back corners.

Hanging Sleeve
Hanging a quilt on the wall is a nice way to display it, but take care to protect the quilt by hanging it properly.

Only a sturdy quilt should be hung. If a quilt is fragile, hanging will only hasten its deterioration. Never use nails, staples, or tacks to hang a quilt.

The hanging method most often used is to slip a dowel or curtain rod through a sleeve sewn to the backing. This distributes the weight evenly across the width of the quilt.

To make a sleeve, cut an 8"-wide strip of leftover backing fabric that is the same length as the quilt edge.

1. Turn under ½" on each end of the strip; then turn under another ½". Topstitch to hem both ends. With wrong sides facing, fold the fabric in half lengthwise and stitch the long edges together. Press seam allowances open and to the middle of the sleeve.

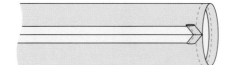

2. Center the sleeve on the quilt 1" below the binding with its seam against the backing. Hand-sew the sleeve to the quilt through backing and batting along both long edges. For large quilts, make two or three sleeve sections so you can use more nails to support the dowel.

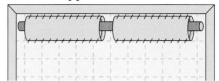

Care & Cleaning

Always shield your quilts from direct light and heat, dust, damp, cigarette smoke, and aerosol sprays. The following suggestions for display, storage, and cleaning are suitable for most quilts. A museum-quality heirloom or fragile antique may have special needs; if you have such a quilt, get expert advice on its care.

Washing

Wash your quilts only when absolutely necessary. Often, a good airing is all that's needed to freshen a quilt. Vacuuming with a hose removes dust. Dry cleaning is not recommended for quilts because it leaves harmful chemicals in the fabric.

When you must wash a quilt, use a mild soap such as Ensure or Orvis Paste. These soaps are available at quilt shops and from mail-order catalogs (see page 144).

If you know that a quilt's fabrics were prewashed and tested for colorfastness, you can wash the quilt as described below. If you're not sure, soak a corner of the quilt in lukewarm water to be sure dyes do not bleed.

A Good Soak. If fabrics are prewashed, you can wash your quilt in the washing machine if the machine is large enough to accommodate the quilt. Use cold or lukewarm water and let the machine run through its normal cycles. Never use bleach.

If your quilt is too large for the machine, wash it in the bathtub, letting it soak in warm, soapy water for about 15 minutes. Rinse repeatedly to remove the soap. Squeeze as much water out of the quilt as possible, but don't wring or twist it.

Drying. Carefully lift the quilt out of the tub, supporting it in your arms so that no part of the quilt is pulled or stressed by the weight of the water. Lay the quilt flat between two layers of towels, and roll it up to remove as much water as possible.

Let the quilt dry flat on the floor. If you want to dry it outside, pick a shady spot on a dry day, and place the quilt between sheets to protect it. When the quilt is almost dry, and if it isn't too large, you can put it in the dryer on a cool setting to smooth out wrinkles and fluff it up.

Putting a wet quilt in a clothes dryer is not recommended, because heat and agitation can damage fabric and batting.

Fading

All fabrics fade over time. Some fade faster and more drastically than others, and there's no sure way to identify those fabrics beforehand. However, here is a simple test that is worthwhile if you have time before making a quilt.

Cut a 4" square of each fabric. Tape the squares to a sunny windowpane. After 18 days, compare them to the remaining yardage. If the squares are faded to the same degree, you can assume the finished quilt will keep a uniform appearance as it ages. If one fabric fades more than the others, you might want to select another for your quilt.

A Breath of Air

By changing the quilt on your bed regularly, you can reduce the damage that exposure will cause to any one quilt. Rotate quilts with the change of each season, for their own good as well as for a fresh look.

All quilts collect dust. Before you put a quilt away for the season, shake it and air it outdoors. A breezy, overcast day is best if the humidity is low. Lay towels on the grass or over a railing; then spread the quilt over the towels. Keep the quilt away from direct sunlight.

Storage

Store quilts in a cool, dry place. Winter cold and summer heat make most attics, basements, and garages inappropriate storage areas.

If you keep a quilt on a rack or in a chest, put several layers of muslin or acid-free paper between the quilt and the wood. A quilt should not be in contact with wood for a long time, as the natural acids in wood will eventually stain the cloth.

To store your quilt, wrap it in a cotton sheet, pillowcase, or acid-free tissue paper (see Mail-Order Resources, page 144). These materials let air circulate but still protect the quilt from dust and damp. Place crumpled acid-free tissue paper inside each fold to prevent stains and creases from developing along fold lines.

Do not store quilts in plastic, which traps moisture and encourages the growth of mildew.

Each time you put a quilt away, fold it differently to prevent damage where fabric fibers become cracked and weak. If possible, avoid folds altogether by rolling the quilt around a tube covered with a cotton sheet.

Glossary

Appliqué. From the French word appliquer, meaning "to lay on," the process of sewing prepared fabric pieces onto a background fabric to create a layered, pictorial design. Also refers to one piece of the appliqué design.

Backing. The bottom layer of a finished quilt. Can be a single width of fabric or pieced.

Basting. Lines of large, temporary stitches that hold the layers of a quilt together for quilting.

Batting. A soft filling between the patchwork top and the backing.

Bearding. Migration of batting fibers through the quilt top or backing.

Between. A short, small-eyed needle used for hand quilting. Available in several sizes, indicated by numbers; the higher the number, the shorter the needle.

Bias. The diagonal of a woven fabric, which runs at a 45° angle to the selvage. This direction has the most stretch, making it ideal for appliqué shapes and for binding curved edges.

Binding. A narrow strip of folded fabric that covers the raw edges of a quilt after it is quilted.

Bleeding. The run-off of dye when fabric is wet.

Chain piecing. Machine sewing in which units are sewn one after the other without lifting the presser foot or cutting thread between units.

Charm quilt. A quilt composed of one shape in many fabrics. Traditionally, no two pieces are the same fabric.

Contrast. The difference in lightness and darkness of color or size of print.

Cross-hatching. Lines of quilting that form a grid of squares or diamonds.

Crosswise grain. Fabric threads woven from selvage to selvage. Crosswise grain has some stretch, but not as much as bias.

Diagonal corners. A quick-piecing technique that results in a contrasting triangle sewn to one or more corners of a square or rectangle. See page 128 for instructions. Also known as snowball corners.

Easing. A technique used to make unequal pieces match at seams by distributing fullness. See page 127.

Fat eighth. A 9" x 22" cut rather than a standard ⅛ yard (4½" x 44").

Fat quarter. An 18" x 22" cut rather than a standard ¼ yard (9" x 44").

Finished size. Dimensions of a piece or unit when all sides are sewn.

Flying Geese. A basic building block of patchwork, this unit is made of two small triangles sewn to short legs of one large triangle.

Four-Patch. A block made of four squares or units, joined in two rows of two squares each.

Four-triangle square. A pieced square made of four right triangles. Also called an Hourglass block.

Grain. The lengthwise and crosswise threads from which fabric is woven. See page 122.

Half-square triangle. A right triangle that results when a fabric square is cut in half diagonally. These triangles are straight grain on the short legs and bias on the hypotenuse.

Hanging sleeve. A fabric casing on the back of a quilt through which a dowel is inserted to hang the quilt on a wall. See page 141.

In-the-ditch. Quilting stitches worked very close to or in the seam line.

Lengthwise grain. Fabric threads parallel to the selvage. Lengthwise grain has very little stretch, if any. Many quiltmakers prefer to cut borders and straight-grain binding on the lengthwise grain.

Nesting. When seam allowances of matching seams fall in opposite directions so that they nest, or fit into one another.

Nine-Patch. A block made of nine squares or units, joined in three rows of three squares each.

Outline quilting. A line of quilting that parallels a seam line, ¼" away.

Pin matching. Using straight pins to align two seams so that they will meet precisely when a joining seam is stitched. $\longrightarrow$

Prairie points. Triangles made from folded squares of fabric that are sewn into seams, creating a dimensional effect. Most often used as an edging.

Quarter-square triangle. The right triangle that results when a fabric square is cut in quarters diagonally, in an X. These triangles are bias on the short legs and straight grain on the hypotenuse. Triangles on the outside edge of a diagonal set are cut in this manner to keep the quilt edge on the straight grain.

Quick piecing. One of several machine-sewing techniques that eliminate or reduce some marking and cutting steps.

Quilt top. The upper layer of a quilt sandwich, it can be pieced, appliqué, or wholecloth. Quilting designs are marked and stitched on the top.

Quilting hoop. A portable wooden frame, round or oval, used to hold small portions of a quilt taut for quilting. A quilting hoop is deeper than an embroidery hoop to accommodate the thickness of the quilt layers. Other types of quilting frames, both portable and stationary, are available in a variety of shapes, sizes, and materials.

Quilting stitch. A running stitch that holds the three layers (top, batting, and backing) of a quilt together.

Quilting thread. Heavier than sewing thread, most brands are designed not to snag or snarl.

Reversed patch. A patchwork piece that is a mirror image of another. To cut a reversed patch, turn the template over (reverse it).

Sashing. Strips of fabric sewn between blocks. Also known as lattice stripping.

Sawtooth. A border treatment consisting of two-triangle squares that creates a jagged look.

Selvage. The finished edge of a woven fabric. More tightly woven than the rest of the fabric, selvage is not used for sewing because it shrinks differently when washed.

Set pieces. Elements of a quilt that separate blocks, such as alternate squares, sashing, or side triangles in a diagonal set.

Set-in seam. Where three seams come together in a Y, one piece is set into the two that create the opening.

Straight grain. The horizontal and vertical threads of a woven fabric. Lengthwise grain runs parallel to the selvage. Crosswise grain is perpendicular to the selvage.

Strip piecing. A quick-piecing technique in which strips of fabric are joined and then cut into segments that become units of a block.

Strip set. A combination of two or more joined strips. These are cut into small segments that become units of patchwork.

Template. A duplicate of a printed pattern, made of sturdy material, that is traced to mark the pattern shape onto fabric.

Triangle-square. A patchwork square made of two or four triangles. When two triangles are joined to make a square, these are called two-triangle squares. When four triangles are joined to make a square, these are called four-triangle squares. Triangles should be cut and sewn so that the straight grain falls on the square's outer edge.

Two-triangle square. A pieced square made of two right triangles. See technique for quick-pieced two-triangle squares on page 130.

Value. The relative lightness or darkness of a color.

Walking foot. A sewing machine foot used for machine quilting and, sometimes, for applying binding. A walking foot feeds a quilt more evenly than a regular foot does.